# DOMESTIC LIFE IN ENGLAND

**Weidenfeld and Nicolson**
London

# NORAH LOFTS

# DOMESTIC LIFE IN ENGLAND

ISBN 0 297 77157 4

*House editor Esther Jagger*
*Layout by Sandra Shafee. Designed by Andrew Shoolbred for*
George Weidenfeld and Nicolson Limited
11 St John's Hill, London SW11

*Filmset by Keyspools Limited, Golborne, Lancashire*
*Printed in Great Britain by Morrison & Gibb Limited Edinburgh*

942 LOF

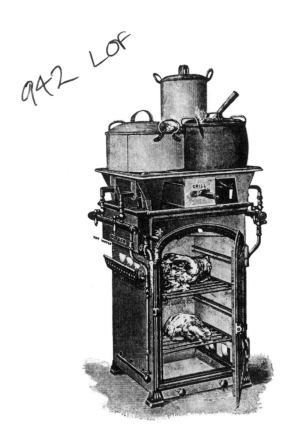

# Contents

1  Cottage and Castle  8

2  The Medieval Tapestry  42

3  Merrie England  80

4  Puritans and Periwigs  112

5  The Age of Elegance  134

6  Poverty and Affluence  170

7  The Equalizing Age  206

Further Reading  245

Acknowledgments  247

Index  249

To all the good women who are living
and the memory of those who are dead,
who over the years have kept my domestic life
on the right lines, leaving my hands free
for the typewriter.

# 1 Cottage and Castle

he question is – where to begin? The choice is dauntingly wide; for domestic means 'concerning the home' and there have been homes in England for as long as there have been people. Even nomads have homes of a kind. Once the camp site is selected, the fire alight, food being cooked and children attended to, the firelit area, comparatively warm, comparatively safe, is a home, if only for a night.

To select the Norman Conquest of 1066 as a starting point may seem arbitrary, even perhaps trite, but there are reasons for it. The Conquest brought England into closer touch with Europe than it had been since the fall of Rome; it brought political, social and linguistic changes; it brought about the use of stone as a common building material, and some of those early stone structures survive to this day. It is possible to stand by an ancient smoke-blackened niche and think 'Somebody cooked here'. You climb the twisting stone stairs and think how difficult they must have been for pregnant women, for young children, for the old and the infirm. You look at the windows and feel how coldly – before glazing was common – the wind must have blown.

Such fancies can only be indulged in what remains of a Norman castle. Examples of purely domestic buildings of the period are extremely rare. If a castle seems out of place when domestic life is under scrutiny it must be remembered that for many people the castle was home. The man in charge, his family, his retainers and servants, all lived there, and at the heart of a military establishment domestic life pursued its quiet, inexorable way. Nothing remains of other homes. The clod cottage crumbled and fell back into the earth from which it was made. The wooden buildings decayed, prey to the ravages of wind and weather, dry rot, wet rot, woodworm and fire.

There had, of course been buildings of durable material erected in England long before the Conquest. The Romans had used stone, marble and brick; but between their departure and the arrival of the Normans there was a gap of roughly 600 years and the people who made their homes in England during that time had little use for what the Romans had left. Angles, Jutes, Saxons and Danes, presently to meld into English, tended to avoid the sophisticated towns and the

OPPOSITE The grim and gaunt exterior of a Norman castle – Rochester Castle, Kent.

comfortable country villas. They came from the part of Europe that had not been touched by Rome; temples and theatres, forums, tessellated floors, baths, underfloor heating, water conveyed by aqueducts and pipes were all alien to their way of life. Avoided and neglected, the Roman buildings fell, were silted over, grown over, and eventually ploughed over, awaiting the archaeologist's trowel, and the English built with wood. The greatest English lord was content with a hall of wood not unlike a barn, with the fire in the middle of the floor, the smoke swirling round until it escaped through a hole in the roof.

It was left to the Normans to erect buildings of stone, which made two innovations possible – in the hall, a fireplace in one wall; and in the kitchen, an oven. But such changes came very gradually and ovens did not become commonplace in cottages for centuries. In fact, well within living memory it was a common sight on Sunday morning to see joints, carefully labelled, being carried along to the nearest bakehouse, to be reclaimed by the fastest moving member of the family at dinner time.

The first stone buildings the Normans raised were naturally castles, to assert their power over the defeated but still hostile English. After William's invasion, as Ordericus Vitalis wrote, 'the native inhabitants were crushed, imprisoned, disinherited, banished and scattered beyond the limits of their own country; while his own vassals and adherents were exalted to wealth and honours and raised to all offices of state.' This new ruling class built nearly fifty castles by the time the *Domesday Book* was written in 1086, and at least another thirty-five were built before 1100. Only the Tower of London and Colchester, Pevensey and Chepstow castles were originally built in stone; the others were built in wood for the sake of speed and rebuilt in stone in the next century. The first castles were usually built on the simple 'motte and bailey' pattern. The last defence was a wooden tower on a high motte or mound. Around the motte ran a moat and beyond this was the bailey, an area surrounded by earth or wooden ramparts. When the castle was rebuilt in stone a large keep surmounted the motte, with three or four storeys providing accommodation for the lord, his family and his retainers. High walls with a strong gateway surrounded the bailey, which was sometimes divided into two wards.

As a centre for domestic life the castle had many drawbacks – the

chief of which was lack of privacy. The hall was the centre of communal life in the daytime, and at night guests of rank shared the host's sleeping space as naturally as they shared his table. The curtains which were part of every well furnished bed had another purpose than the exclusion of draughts. Some castles did provide a retreat for women and young children, called the solar, but it was not until the end of the Middle Ages, when security was no longer the prime function of a building, that domestic comfort was sought after.

The manor house which was the home of lesser lords or knights was still built of wood in the early Middle Ages, though often on stone foundations. It must have been as cold, damp and smoky as the homes of the villagers but the building would have been stronger and more spacious. The better cottages had a wooden framework with walls

The keep of Ludlow Castle, with its typical rounded Norman arches (right – the pointed ones are of later date). The windows would have been as bereft of glass as they are now.

'When Adam delved
and Eve span, who
was then a
gentleman?' This
delightful early
illumination of Adam
and Eve gives us a
good idea of peasant
family life. Note the
heavily swaddled
child in the carved
wooden cradle.

made by packing a mixture of clay, dung and straw over a frame of wattle laths; the worst were low hovels of clay and stone. The wooden homes were pitiably vulnerable to fire, and to guard against fire breaking out in the night when a household was asleep, a law was passed ordering the raking out or damping down of all fires before retiring. Because the law came to be known as curfew – a corruption of *couvrefeu* – it is often regarded as a Norman innovation, but earlier rulers, amongst them Alfred the Great, had also imposed it. William of Normandy merely revived and enforced it. It was not then regarded as the punitive measure that it is today. One way of guarding against the risk of a fire flaring up or emitting sparks during the night was to cover it with freshly hacked lumps of turf with the damp soil still clinging to them. It is interesting to note that when in the nineteenth century the kitchen range came into use the device which controlled the rate at which it burned was called a damper.

Twenty years after the Conquest only two major estates were still in English hands. The gulf between castle and cottage was therefore not only in riches and status but in nationality and language; it was 300 years before English replaced French as the language of government and the ruling class. The gulf in status had widened with the coming of the Normans who imposed the feudal system on the freer Anglo-Saxon society. Many peasants who had been poor but free under Edward the Confessor became villeins or bondsmen under the new lords, forced among other duties to work a certain number of days on the lord's demesne as rent for their own few strips, unable to leave the manor to seek better conditions, unable even to marry without permission.

The cottage woman shared her husband's labour on the land as well as seeing to the feeding and clothing of the family. Fortunately, purely household duties were light. The cottage usually consisted of a single room in which the whole family lived, ate and slept; the floor was of hard-trodden bare earth, the furniture minimal – a table, a few stools (all home-made), and a straw-stuffed mattress. In hard weather any small animal owned by the family, usually a pig or a goat, would be brought in at night, both for its own protection and for the heat that it could contribute to a place which, once the meagre central fire was doused, soon grew chilly.

The cottage fire had to be used for many purposes – cooking and smoking the pig after it had been killed, as well as for foot- and boot-warming.

Cooking was necessarily simple; most of it was done in the single iron pot which could be either suspended above the fire, or perched upon the stones which surrounded the shallow hollow where the fire lay. The pot seldom contained meat. More often it held oatmeal gruel, dumplings made of flour and water, or any vegetable that was available – cabbages, onions, leeks, peas and beans, as well as many things now regarded as weeds, such as nettles, dandelions, wild sorrel, and even ground elder. What came out of the black pot was likely to be a mess. In the authorised version of the Bible Esau sold his birthright for 'a mess of pottage'; a group of nuns who ate together was known as a mess; and officers in the armed forces use the word still.

When the black pot in the cottage saw meat it was pig meat. The pig was always the poor man's friend because its production rate was high and like man and rat it was omnivorous – it would eat anything, even, if hard-pressed, its own young. For most of the year it could forage for itself and did particularly well in autumn when acorns fell from oak trees and nuts from beeches. On many manors the peasants had the right to pannage – permission for pigs to go a certain distance, on certain days of the year, into the otherwise forbidden woods. The pig of this period was a leaner, rangier animal than that of the present day, but it was at its best just at the time when all but the necessary breeding stock was slaughtered.

Nothing was wasted. The blood was caught and mixed with oatmeal or coarse barley flour, flavoured with whatever was handy and made into black pudding, a dish still popular in the north of England. The gut, well washed out, made a natural skin for sausages; pigs' trotters could be served whole, or, with other bits and pieces, converted into brawn. Some joints could be eaten fresh, boiled or roasted on a makeshift spit, but with the hungry days of winter looming, as much as possible had to be preserved by salting or smoking. In the cottage with no amenities such preservation was a hit-or-miss process and may have bequeathed us the term 'to save one's bacon', meaning a narrow escape. Meat preserved in such elementary fashion was tough and took a lot of chewing. 'Chawbacon' was for centuries a term of contempt. As a final contribution to the welfare of those who had owned him in life, the dead pig gave any fat he had acquired. A little grease in a shallow container, with a few twisted strands of linen thread afloat in it, yielded a dim light for those who could not afford a candle or even a rush dip. Except when someone was ill and needed attention the peasant household had no need of artificial light. Dawn to dusk constituted the ordinary working day. At dusk they slept.

In the matter of foresight, of providing for the future, the Norman lady in the castle had an enormous advantage over the woman in the cottage. She had space. Many of those dark underground rooms regarded by the eager sightseer as dungeons were actually storerooms, stocked with provisions against siege. The cottage woman had no storage room – at most a kind of shelf at the far end of her hovel, and even that sometimes encroached upon by sleeping children.

One commodity which was most carefully stored in all households was salt. In the castle kitchen with its hearth in the wall a niche would be made and reserved for the purpose. Later, when even humble homes had a hearth to one side, they had niches too, and people who restore old cottages nowadays often find them when the original fireplace is exposed. They bear a singular, and perhaps symbolic, resemblance to the niches designed to hold holy images. In the very early cottage, with its fire in the centre of the floor, and its walls of clod or wattle and daub, the keeping of so hygroscopic an article as salt must have been a problem. Perhaps the family salt box sat by the stones around the hearth. Salt was one of the few necessities that could not be provided by the village community. It had to be brought in from the coast, where sea water was evaporated, or from places like Cheshire where it could be mined. This made it an expensive commodity. The *Domesday Book* describes how fines were charged in Cheshire to prevent the carriers overloading their cart or horse with salt: 'Anyone who so loaded his cart that the axle broke within a league of either Wich paid 2 shillings to the king's officer or the earl's if he could be undertaken within a league. Similarly he who so loaded a horse as to break its back paid 2 shillings. . . .'

Wattle and daub construction. The wooden beams (right) formed the 'skeleton' on to which wattle (centre) was attached. The gaps in between were then filled in with mud 'daub'. It seems a primitive technique, but there are wattle and daub cottages still standing today.

The importance of salt is reflected in many ways. It was unlucky to spill salt. That may have been an invented superstition to prevent careless handling; or it may have been fact in an age when servants and children were freely chastised. To eat a man's salt and then act against him was regarded as dastardly behaviour. To describe a person as the salt of the earth is still high praise; to say that he is not worth his salt, exactly the reverse. The salt tax was a valuable source of revenue. Streets and roads were named after this one commodity. A salary – derived from the Latin word for salt, since Roman soldiers were paid in salt – is still regarded as superior to a wage; and to have something salted away means having money saved. Except perhaps for bread no article in common use has left such a mark on the English language. A man's breeding could be judged by his behaviour towards the salt at table; it was extremely uncouth to dig into the salt bowl with a knife that had not previously been wiped on bread or napkin. The salt container at the rich man's table was often the most elaborate thing upon it; it could be made of silver or silver gilt, decorated with enamel or mother of pearl; and one's place in relationship to it was a status symbol one sat above, or below the salt.

The cottage woman preserved what she could of her pig. The castle had wider resources. Cattle – again with the exception of some breeding animals – were killed in autumn and their flesh salted away. The only winter feed then known was hay, and that was needed for the work-oxen and for the horses. Horses, being indispensable cogs in the military regime, had priority, and the oxen often emerged from their winter retirement too weak to pull a plough; and so, sometimes, did the men who owned them.

We tend to think of scurvy as a sailors' disease but it was rife among the poor in those faraway winters. The well-to-do suffered less, for their diet was less restricted to food lacking in essential vitamins. The spoils of the hunt – deer, wild boar and hare – provided fresh food, and so did the carp pool and the dovecote. The lord of the manor could afford to keep a cow through the winter and ensure a supply of fresh milk; he could also indulge in the uneconomic practice of eating a pig before it had attained its maximum growth. Falconry, like hunting, was a sport, but it provided some edible tit-bits; there were pheasants and

Hawking – the pastime of the rich – offered the bonus of delicious tit-bits to add to the castle menu.

partridges, all by right the lord's. While the cottager ate salt meat and bread the cook in the castle kitchen might be preparing a well-stuffed bird; inside a young cockerel a pheasant; inside the pheasant a partridge, and inside the partridge a quail, snipe or woodcock.

Scurvy, beginning with lack of energy and proceeding to loss of sight, spongy gums, and underskin haemorrhages – the dread 'blew spottes' – was not understood, but the cure was known; anything fresh could work a near miracle. Spring was the season when fresh stuff began to grow, and a form of grass known as scurvy grass was eagerly sought and devoured. So were the earliest green shoots on the haw-thorns. Only fifty years ago country children still pounced on the first hawthorn leaves and ate them, calling them bread and cheese. The poor country man could seek the life-restoring greenstuff at the wood's edge, along the baulks – or banks – which divided one hold-ing from another in the great fields. His fellow in the town had to go further afield and some old maps show, just where the houses end, a lane called Scurvy Lane. The name does not appear on later maps, for being associated with poverty and misery the word became derogatory and has survived in that sense – a scurvy knave; a scurvy trick.

It may not be without significance that the first poem in the *Oxford Book of English Verse* is neither pious nor lovelorn; it is a greeting to that not altogether admirable bird, the cuckoo – herald of the spring; proof that those who had survived, in however poor condition, might hope to see another summer.

> Sumer is icumen in,
> Llude sing cuccu!
> Groweth sed, and bloweth med,
> And springeth the wude nu –
>   Sing cuccu!

This aspect of eleventh-century life may appear to be over-grim to those whose backward glance reaches no farther than the later medieval period when Chaucer's 'poure widewe' woman owned three large sows, three kine, a sheep, a cock and seven hens. But at the time in question, immediately after the Conquest, England was a subdued country under stern rule. A provident peasant might rear a few geese,

but the lord of the manor could take them if he felt so inclined. To whom could the wronged man complain of injustice? To the manorial court, presided over by the lord himself?

Except in large towns, of which there were few, all bread was made at home and varied in quality and colour, from almost black to off-white. The poor man's loaf would be made of rye or barley flour, containing the whole grain and, since methods of threshing were primitive, a good deal of the husk as well. Such bread was nourishing, but it was coarse and dark, and in rye bread there lurked an unrecognized danger. Rye is the favourite host of a fungus called ergot which, taken in sufficient quantities, can make pregnant women miscarry, and in men, women and children can produce a serious, if temporary, nervous disorder. People suffering from ergot poisoning – again mainly the poor – appeared to go mad, rushing about aimlessly, performing strange antics, shouting incoherently, laughing hysterically, and constantly scratching. The complaint produced intolerable itching and burning sensations all over the body and for that reason was known as St Antony's Fire. With the decline in the use of rye as a staple cereal, the affliction became rarer. The last outbreak of epidemic size occurred in France in 1816, but isolated outbreaks are still known.

For others, catching food was a more serious matter – here is a novel way of trapping rabbits with the aid of a ferret. Interestingly, the whole operation seems to have been carried out by women.

Peasants reaping corn, closely supervised by the reeve.

The peasant ploughed, sowed, reaped and harvested his own grain crop and his lord's, but it was illegal for the peasant woman to pound it into flour in her quern – a kind of pestle and mortar device. It must go to the mill, for the mill belonged to the overlord, and paid a special tax. It is unlikely that the peasant paid the miller in money for this service. Coin money was in short supply at the time and very little of it found its way into the hands of the oppressed people. The miller took his payment in kind – a tithe or some other measure of the flour.

The flour used in the castle kitchen was more often of wheat. Some of it passed through a succession of sieves, growing paler with each sieving; but the germ remained and the most delicate white bread of the time – manchet bread – was probably the colour of the modern wholemeal loaf. It was not for general consumption; one's place in the castle hierarchy determined the quality of the bread one ate, and even at the privileged high table there was a distinction between the kinds of bread served. A slab of coarse 'trencher' bread, at least four days old, often took the place of a plate. A piece of more delicate bread was placed by the trencher's side. Hungry people ate the trencher bread too. Those with more delicate appetites left the trencher – now well soaked with gravy – to be collected in a basket and given to the poor.

In the castle bread could be baked in the oven; in the cottage it would be roasted on the stones surrounding the fire and would need constant attention. The story of Alfred the Great allowing his attention to wander and so allowing the poor woman's cakes to burn may be legendary, but it presents a vivid picture of this method of cooking. In all probability they were cakes of bread, for the ingredients necessary for cake in the modern sense of the word would be out of reach to the poor and not plentiful even in the kitchen of a rich household.

The oven which the stone wall of a castle made possible was of a design which lasted, with only the slightest of variations, for 800 years. Many examples can still be seen in the kitchens of old farmhouses. Basically it was a hole in a fireproof wall, fitted with an iron door. Into this oven went a good sheaf of wood, some thin twigs for quick ignition, and some that were more solid and capable of generating more heat. The stone – later the bricks – of the oven's lining absorbed the heat, and by the time the wood had burned to ash, the oven was ready for use. The ash was hastily raked out, or pushed to one side, and what was to be cooked was placed inside; bread went to the back, and pies and pastry dishes which took less time to cook were put in the front so that they could be taken out without disturbing the bread. (Pastry, incidentally, was for the rich; the four and twenty blackbirds baked in a pie was a dish fit to set before a king. The present-day Anglo-Saxon may shrink from the idea of eating song birds; our forebears were less squeamish, and even now *pâté de merle* is served as a great delicacy in some restaurants on the Continent.)

The walls of the oven gave back the heat they had absorbed. It was an equitable heat, and self-regulating; everything went into what cookery books call a sharp oven, and then the heat gradually declined. What remained of warmth when all the food was withdrawn was not wasted; the cooling oven could be used for airing clothes, for drying fruit, for melting tallow. The superiority of the oven over hearthside cooking is evidenced in the word bakemeats, for years associated with such important occasions as weddings and funerals. In time, communal ovens were set up in villages. Placed well away from any combustible building, this form of outdoor oven resembled a beehive.

The difference between very good bread and very bad bread depended upon the quality of the flour, the method of cooking, and upon a third element, the leavening or raising, the activating enzyme known as yeast. Anything which would ferment would serve to 'leaven the lump', in the biblical phrase. Here again the peasant woman with her lack of space and her limited resources would be at a disadvantage, and probably most of her bread cakes were flat – the unleavened bread of the Passover. One form of yeast was the by-product of brewing and winemaking, or even of stewed fruit kept long enough to ferment. This frothy, volatile stuff could be rendered dormant and more durable if it were spread out on a board and allowed to dry. A solid block of yeast could be built up by adding layer to layer. In the cramped cottage such a process would take up too much space and time, and the breadmaker there, when she used yeast, reserved a small piece of leavened dough and used it to activate the next batch. The same method was used by American frontiersmen centuries later and gained them the nickname of Sourdough.

The white, well-raised loaf became such a symbol of privilege that it has affected the eating habits of the nation to the present day. White was best; the whiter the better. When breadmaking became an industry, the bakers recognized this prejudice, and, until forbidden by law, whitened their loaves by the use of additives such as alum and chalk. Some early food reformers accused bakers of using ground bonemeal: 'I'll grind his bones to make my bread!' But the demand for the whiter than white loaf continued and has not yet halted.

The cook in the castle, with an oven at his command, could make pastry, and since cooking, once freed from the necessity of feeding the greatest possible number of mouths at the least possible expense, becomes an art, the cook delighted himself by making things as pleasing to the eye as to the palate. He was handicapped by the lack of something regarded as essential today – sugar. He had native fruits, either dried in the cooling oven to be reconstituted by soaking, or fruit preserved in honey. He could make tarts and pies, and because pastry put into a hot oven retained its shape, he could make very decorative dishes. To this day the raised pork pie is edged with something much resembling the battlements of a castle, and that most delectable of cakes, the cream horn, is a memorial to the ancient horns which called men to battle – or pigs from their gorging. Plainer pastry shapes to contain meat, fruit or custard, were called coffins – less morbid a name than it sounds, since it was in fact a version of coffer.

In addition to enjoying better cooking facilities and a wider range of basic materials, the cook in a wealthy household had access to spices. They were extremely costly because they had made a long journey before they ended in a carefully guarded spice chest in an English household. Along the route known as the Spice Road, which began farther east than India, cinnamon, cloves, nutmeg, ginger, pepper and a small quantity of sugar had been transported by many different means, and passed through many hands, each handler making some profit. Much of the fabulous wealth of Venice was derived from this trade for Venice was the terminus of the Spice Road, and a dispersal point. Most of the exotic stuff which reached England had made

Merchants waiting eagerly for cargoes to arrive in port.

another, overland journey to reach the ports of the Low Countries to which it was equally profitable. One of the earliest recognized organizations for mutual support and the regulation of prices and weights was that of the Pepperers; it was established in the same year that William the Conqueror took England. Because its members – dealers in minute quantities of precious stuff – had to be precise, they were entrusted with the regulation of other weights and measures, the 'Grossari', and became known as grocers. Their counterparts in France were not re-christened; the grocer's shop in France, if still in private hands, is the *épicerie*.

Over-indulgence in highly spiced food was believed to be unhealthy because it made the blood hot; and, with nice consistency, a mug of ale or a cup of wine, warmed and sprinkled with a pinch of spice, was regarded as a sovereign remedy for a chill. Those who could afford to do so added spices to the brine in which meat was preserved, but perhaps the most important function served by spices – notably pepper – was to disguise the taste of tainted meat. There are sinister hints about how to deal with meat badly preserved or kept too long in the cask: it could be improved by being well washed in vinegar; or if it were so far gone as to be green, burial in the earth for two days might restore it to edibility. A last resort, for those who could afford it, was a good dash of

BELOW A scullion turns roasting birds on a spit, while another adds wood to the fire.

OPPOSITE The cook chops up a roast sucking pig with a very sinister-looking knife (left), and (right) his very un-dainty efforts are carried in to the hall to be served.

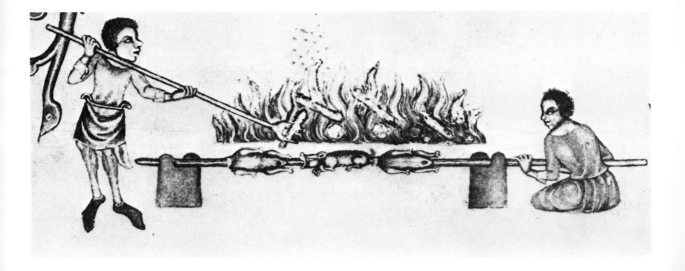

pepper, and the pepperpot, in shape singularly similar to the modern one, held, after the salt container, pride of place on the well furnished table.

The main meat dish was still cooked in the most primitive way of all, by exposure to an open fire. The spit was a refinement of the age-old method of holding raw meat towards the heat, cooking unevenly and losing the juices and the fat. It consisted of a bar upon which the whole animal or joints of it were impaled, and rested upon two upright stands with heavy bases and y-shaped tops; it could be turned so that the meat would cook evenly. The spit stood beside the fire, not over it, and the juices and fat fell into a wide dripping pan just below it. Dripping had value in an age when butter was not plentiful and margarine not yet dreamed of – it could be eaten spread on bread; used in pastry-making; or for basting other spitted meats with little fat of their own, such as pheasants, venison or veal. And if there happened to be a surplus it could always be given away to the poor.

Sometimes the spit was turned by a small boy whose task it was; to shield himself from the fierce heat of the fire he would hold up a wet blanket, or an old straw arrow target. Some spits were mechanized, with a cogged wheel and a weight at the end of a string; some had a handle, long enough to be turned outside the full glare of the fire.

And some again were powered by dogs paddling away at a kind of treadmill.

Of all the fat that fell from the spitted joint, that from mutton was most valued, for it had another very important use. It set hard and could be used for making candles. It takes an effort of the imagination – or a cut in the electricity supply – to make us realize how important a part the candle played in the lives of our forebears. The game not being worth the candle is no idle expression.

The poor household had rushdips. They consisted of reeds, stripped, and the pith dipped once or twice into mutton fat, enough to make it stand upright and give a little light for a short time. In grander houses candlemaking was a long, slow and important process. A special board was used, with holes at regular intervals, and through the holes twisted linen threads were suspended. The board was lowered over a dish containing mutton fat which clung to the linen wick and made it rigid; the force of gravity pulled each embryo candle straight. The process was repeated until the dangling candles had taken on the desired thickness. But care had to be taken not to make them too thick; an over-stout candle meant that the outer edge melted more slowly than the part near the wick and formed a cup, so that the wick drowned in a puddle of grease.

Even the best-made candle of this kind exuded a smell of burnt fat. There were other and better candles, made of beeswax, but they were for palaces and churches. In the time immediately after the Conquest, piety was as much the fashion as respectability was to become in a later age. Men of violent, bloodthirsty natures would build and endow churches, and bequeath vast acres to monastic establishments; the women contributed clear-burning wax candles, embroidered altar cloths and splendid ceremonial garments for the priests. Many castles had their own private chapel as well, served by a resident chaplain.

Candles were also needed out of doors; they were then shielded from the wind and rain by a metal cage with panels of finely shaved horn which gave the device its name – lanthorn, or lantern. The not over-bright light of one candle, obscured by the only half-transparent horn, must have made moving about in a yard or stable or castle precincts a perilous business, and summer was welcomed for the longer hours of daylight as well as the other benefits it brought. Even making a light was a tedious business unless one were near a fire, in which case a dry twig could convey the flame; otherwise people had to resort to the tinder box and the immemorial process of making a spark by striking flint and iron together and thus inducing a piece of very dry linen to smoulder, puffing at it until it broke into flame which could be transferred. We do much the same thing every time we use a cigarette lighter, but what that spark ignites is far more inflammable than a tinder rag, however dry.

In the cottage the dinner table was always bare and there was neither space enough nor time enough to allow any formality about meals. In the castle it was otherwise, and the preparing of a table was almost a ritual. In the post-Conquest period even the lord's own table was not a permanent thing, consisting only of trestles and boards. These were set up and covered with a woollen cloth, generally scarlet and often embroidered around the edges which reached down to the floor. Over this were laid two linen cloths, one on top of the other, placed diagonally and in such a way that they did not hide the edges of the scarlet cloth. The need for two white cloths is understandable if we remember the bread trenchers that were in use. There were certain rules regarding the tablecloth – it was unmannerly to wipe one's knife, or one's greasy fingers, upon it; to use it for blowing one's nose was impolite indeed! The existence of such rules proves the necessity.

The first thing to be placed upon the table was the principal salt, which grew more and more decorative and elaborate as the years moved on. When the table was cleared it was the last thing to be removed. Then the drinking vessels were taken from what was literally a cup board; two, sometimes three, shelves against the wall and offering, to the knowing eye, clear evidence of rank and wealth.

One of the simplest and earliest drinking vessels was a hollowed-out horn, but even this could be rimmed and banded, provided with legs so that it could stand on the table, and made of silver and silver gilt, or even of gold. It was gradually replaced by the cup as we know it – the pattern changing little over the years. Godparents still give christening cups, amazingly similar in shape to the early ones; and silver cups are still presented to winners of a contest as they were in tournaments long ago.

Once the salt and the drinking cups were in place the setting of the table was not onerous. Most people carried and used their own knives. There were no forks. The fork as a table implement originated in Italy, became fashionable in France and reached England only in the thirteenth or fourteenth century; though its prototype was in the English kitchen even before the Conquest. It was a one-pronged fork, called a spike, which was used when carving. Spoons were in general use, and made of such varying materials that the phrase 'to be born with a silver spoon in one's mouth' is still a tag of privilege. Some of the wooden spoons, chiefly of boxwood, were beautifully carved, often with a representation of an apostle or a saint on the handle. It is still possible today to buy a set of silver apostle spoons.

What did they drink? To ask that question is to ask the modern mind, however imaginative, to make a difficult jump – no tea, coffee or cocoa; no lemonade, orangeade or mineral waters. There was water, of course. All the Anglo-Saxon villages which had now become Norman manors had been sited within easy reach of a stream; most castles, in readiness for a siege, had their own wells from which reasonably clean and weed-free water could be winched up. There was ale, which was the product of brewing, mainly from barley, without the addition of hops. Hops, when introduced from Flanders, were at first regarded as an adulter-ative. And there was wine of widely differing kinds.

Old maps, old place names and the *Domesday Book* indicate that vines were widely cultivated. It is unlikely that such careful husband-men as the monks in the new stone abbeys would have devoted so much land to a crop that was unrewarding, so in the absence of any hard evidence it may be permissible to think that England was enjoying rather warmer weather in this period. In any case, at a time when almost anything from cowslips to spruce shoots was being made into some kind of alcoholic beverage, even a below-standard grape was not to be despised. In addition to wine there was cider, made from apples; perry, from pears; and the very old English drink, mead, made from honey, and sickly sweet. An old riddle describes the power of

mead to make a man drunk: 'Robbed of his strength, loud in speech, deprived of his might, he has no control over his mind, his feet, or his hands. . . . Discover what I am called who thus binds men upon earth till they are dazed by my blows in the light of the day.'

The triumph of imported wines over the native born may have been due to a change in climate, a change in fashion, or to the fact that Henry II, who came to the throne in 1154, married Eleanor of Aquitaine whose enormous inheritance included some of the best vine-growing districts of France. Trade would be reciprocal; so much good English wool in return for so much wine from the valley of the Loire. We have no reason to suppose that the snob element was less active then than now, and to that element the exotic has irresistible appeal.

Whatever the beverage, glass had no part either in its storing or its serving. It was not that glass was unknown – glass beads have been found in ancient Egyptian tombs; it was simply that it had not yet been fully domesticated. Wine travelled and was stored in casks, and came to table in jugs, some very beautiful both in shape and material. The Norman table itself, however well set and however well served –

OVERLEAF Cutlery and crockery as we know it were quite unknown in Norman times, and no-one objected to eating with his hands, as this portion of the Bayeux Tapestry shows.

DIVM: ET·HIC·EPIS·
P̄OTV̄:BE

with pages and serving boys offering the various dishes, with bowls of water and napkins for the cleansing of hands – was not comfortable. As a general rule people sat on backless benches. The bench with a back – sometimes padded and embroidered – and the chair came later.

Dinner, taken around mid-day, was everywhere the principal meal of the day and everybody was ready for it. Breakfast was – and was to remain for some time – a very scanty meal indeed; a cup of ale, or water, a bit of bread, literally a mere breaking of the night's fast. All able-bodied people had been astir since first light. Most places were within sound of a bell in some religious establishment, and it rang at noon as well as at certain other times during the day. Apart from these bells time-telling must have been a haphazard affair before the invention of clocks and watches. There was of course, the sun-dial, but as one of them truly says, 'I mark only the sunny hours.'

Supper was eaten at six or seven o'clock, the time probably governed by the seasons, and in a poor household it too was a scanty meal. The few surviving lists of foods served in rich households reveal to the amazed modern eye little difference between dinner and supper. They also show that although the meals were divided into courses there was not the distinction between the kinds of food served at each course; meat, poultry, fish and sweetmeats had a place in them all. The choice between boiled mutton and custard must have been hard.

Fish was compulsory eating on Fridays, on fast days and during Lent, and it was more of a penance then than it would be today. The sea teemed with fish but the roads were so bad that it was impossible to get sea fish far inland while still in an edible condition. Most of the fish eaten was salted, all varieties going under the general name of stockfish, or freshwater fish whose flat, muddy taste had to be disguised by sauces. An exception to this was the oyster which could survive in brackish water for as long as twelve days. Oysters, nowadays only for the rich, were plentiful and therefore cheap until comparatively recent times; most excavated Roman villas have piles of oyster shells amongst the other kitchen debris, and Dickens's Sam Weller in *The Pickwick Papers* still called oysters food for the poor. The stinking fish which the adage advises us not to cry was firmly dealt with, less because it was regarded as harmful to health than because

Catching fish for Friday. This fortunate angler's catch would have been considerably fresher than fish that had been transported inland from the coast, over abominable roads.

stench was associated with pestilence. Really stinking fish was confiscated and burned. There were precautions, too, against the taking of immature fish; the mesh of a fishing net must not be too small. Anyone selling undersized fish suffered the suitable punishment of having his illegal wares strung round his neck. In time oysters were regarded as a possibly dwindling asset and were granted a close season from Easter to August – the origin of the still-observed custom that oysters can only be eaten when there is an R in the month.

Fish was so important to the fasting monasteries that they often had their own fishpond. A twelfth-century chronicler at Bury St Edmunds tells a sad tale of the ruthlessness of Abbot Samson:

He raised the level of the fish-pond of Babwell by the new mill to such a height, that owing to the holding up of the waters there is no man rich or poor, having lands by the waterside, from the Towngate to Eastgate, but has lost his garden and orchards. . . . The Cellarer's meadow is ruined, the Infirmarer's orchard is drowned . . . and all the neighbours complain of it. Once the Cellarer spoke to him in full Chapter concerning the greatness of the loss, but the Abbot at once angrily replied that he was not going to lose his fish-pond for the sake of our meadow.

After food, that primary concern, the domesticated woman of whatever rank must look to the clothing of her family. The peasant needed to be shielded against wind and weather, and to have clothes which would not impede his work; once these aims had been attained the style of the cottager's dress remained basically unaltered for centuries – for men hose and a short tunic, for women a plain gown short enough to be clear of the mud. The material was homespun – the fleece of the sheep after it had been through four simple processes: washing, carding, spinning and weaving. It was a dingy greyish buff in colour, and very durable in texture. The woman of the family would wash the wool and then card it. Carding involved dragging a home-made tool or a teazle head through the tangled mass until all the strands lay in the same direction. These were then wound around one end of a stick called the distaff; with a deft finger a few strands of the wool were pulled out and twisted tight, joined by another fingerful and so spun into one continuous thread which a twirl of the distaff made into the equivalent of our ball of wool. Spinning could become an almost automatic process, and since the distaff was neither heavy nor cumbersome a woman could carry it about with her and spin at any time when her hands were not otherwise engaged. The phrase 'the distaff side' of a family is still sometimes used to refer to the female side, and until this century replaced it by the terms bachelor or career girl, and marriage was no longer regarded as the chief ambition of every single girl, spinster was a dread word.

For really bad weather the peasant wore on his head a hood with a very elongated point which could be wrapped around his neck like a scarf. It might also have, if his wife had been diligent, a rudimentary cape, wide enough to give extra protection to his shoulders, but not so wide as to restrict the movements of his arms.

In the castle clothes served another purpose, though protection from cold was still the main objective. The Norman lady guarded herself against draughts with a head-dress of the kind still worn by nuns of certain orders; a wimple covered her head and ears, and its ends were wound about her throat; she wore a high-necked, long-sleeved dress which reached her toes; and over it a mantle which in winter might be edged and even lined with fur. Men were robed in hose with an inner mantle and an over mantle. But the clothes inside the castle differed from those of the poor in their bright colours, created either by dyes or by embroidery.

Dyeing is mentioned as a specialized trade quite early, but the dyers, like bakers, would operate only in towns, and much home-produced cloth was therefore also home-dyed. Most of the dyes were of vegetable origin. A plant distantly related to the wallflower yielded woad, the blue substance which the Ancient Britons had used as a body decoration. Madder provided the red shades; but although its near relative, the field madder, abounded in English fields, the dyers' madder did not flourish here and had to be imported. Saffron – and probably other plants now forgotten – gave yellow; not a very popular colour since it had become associated with the Jews who were steadily more and more disliked, until in 1290 Edward I expelled them altogether. The outer husks of walnuts were widely used, and provided shades ranging from buff through a variety of browns to black. (Steeped in vinegar the husks made ink, too.) Elderberries, blackber-

A dyer at work,
stirring his boiling
vat.

ries and currants yielded very stable colours. To this day one of the
most powerful claims that can be made for any washing powder is that
it will remove fruit stains. Bark from trees was used, too; especially the
bark of oak which was employed in the tanning of leather.

The depth of colour would depend upon the strength of the solution
into which the fabric was plunged, and upon the time allowed for its
absorption; varying shades could be obtained by mixing dyes.
Possibly the most troublesome colour of all, both to attain in the first
place and to maintain afterwards, was simple white. Neither wool nor
linen in its natural state was truly white. Bleaching was a process
known from the earliest civilizations, but like so many things it had
been lost during the so-called Dark Ages. Or perhaps not quite lost –
something had drifted through, some guiding principle, a rule of

thumb. Fabrics could be whitened by soaking them in buttermilk, and then exposing them to the sunshine. The word alkaline had no place in the vocabulary of the time, but buttermilk's bleaching power was known – it had its effect on dairymaids' fingers and on the complexions of those who used it for washing. As for the power of the sun, it could make any colour fade. So the tedious process – into the buttermilk, out into the sun – could go on for weeks on end.

Linen – for personal wear and for domestic use as tablecloths and napkins – was at this time the perquisite of the rich. The peasant woman was not over-concerned with washing days. Homespun, dingy to start with, became soiled and absorbed sweat, but it had that quality which always distinguishes good woollen cloth – it could wear dirty and clean. To this day good tweed, the nearest we have to homespun, is remarkably resistant to the hazards of everyday wear.

Linen, having been made white, must be kept white; and soap, as we know it, was the product of another lost craft. The first-century Roman writer Pliny, willing to observe everything and to write about it, described how soap was made by mixing fat and woodash then hardening it with acid. As with bleaching the exact formula had been lost, but the principle remained and a kind of race memory. Norman linen was washed with a soft mixture of animal fat and the purest, whitest wood ash that the hearth could provide. It was then bleached again, and any household of substance had its own bleaching ground.

Every woman of the time was obliged to be handy with her needle, but most of the embroidery was done by those who had leisure. One superb example of what could be achieved with needle and thread has come down to us in the Bayeux Tapestry, which is not in fact a tapestry but a stitched picture made as a record of the events of 1066. The cold grey stone walls of many a castle and church must have been brightened and given an illusion of warmth by such embroidered hangings; and needles were busy, too, upon the hems and sleeves and armholes of clothes worn by both men and women; on the borders of tablecloths and altar cloths and upon ceremonial ecclesiastical robes. But sumptuous materials such as velvet and differing kinds of silk, though known, were not in general use in the settling down time after the Conquest; nor was there any dramatic change in fashion. The

Normans were practical people, and their clothes were like them.

The Norman lady was a stay-at-home woman, busy in her little sphere and not venturing far outside it, for the state of the roads made travel uninviting to say the least. The Romans had made roads so well that some of the lost ones, excavated 1500 years later, are still sound. With a few remarkable exceptions, the Anglo-Saxons had ignored the Roman roads and made their own foot trails and pony tracks. They were not engineers: unlike the Romans, they would skirt a great tree or an outcrop of rock; and when pack ponies came into general use they chose the easiest way, preferring on rising ground to take the gradient gradually by weaving from side to side. It was the overladen pack pony rather than Chesterton's rolling English drunkard who made the rolling English road. It was unsurfaced and in very bad condition, although certain communities were supposed to keep assigned sections of it in order, mainly by tipping a load of stones into the worst holes. Wheeled traffic was impossible on such roads, so when ladies travelled they rode pillion or in litters suspended between two horses. Wayside inns were so few and so bad that many of the big religious houses had their own hostels where travellers could be accommodated. The temptation to gad about was small and the Norman lady made only necessary journeys, such as family visits or pilgrimages. The peasant woman might spend her life on the one manor; indeed she required permission to leave it.

Life was hard and harsh, lacking in the amenities which we regard as essentials, but people of all ranks escaped the loneliness that afflicts so many in the present age. The cottage might easily house three generations of the same family. The old, even when past work in the fields, could usually contribute something to the general wellbeing; they could mind small children, keep the fire going and the black pot boiling, sew, spin, patch clothes and cobble shoes. (It is surely significant that in Norman times and for centuries afterwards one of the reasons for suspecting a woman to be a witch was that she lived alone; so rare a condition was a sign of something wrong.)

At the other end of the scale were the young who had a very brief childhood, only minimally briefer in the cottage than in the castle. Nowhere was childhood regarded as a condition which needed special consideration or provision. The peasant children, as soon as they were steady on their feet, could find something useful to do, gathering nuts and berries in season, collecting the other edible stuff that grew wild, picking up the little tufts of wool shed by sheep. Later they herded geese and pigs, surreptitiously set snares for rabbits and so graduated, by about the age of ten, into miniature working persons.

The cottages must have been horribly overcrowded, and since there was uncultivated land in plenty, expansion of the village might have been expected. But the times were troubled; people felt safer when huddled together and within easy reach of some large building such as the church or castle where the women and children, at least, could seek refuge. The lord of the manor might be an alien, often tyrannical, usually greedy, but he was also a fighting man, ready to defend his own.

Musicians like these would have played at banquets, to entertain the guests.

Entertainment was
rarely provided in
these early days, and
people had to
provide their own –
by playing chess,
for instance.

Life had its lighter side and there were amusements, though the time
when entertainment was brought to people had not yet arrived.
Strolling minstrels, performing bears and other entertainers were rare
in post-Conquest days, for their very existence postulates a freedom to
move about. Manorial life had a static quality. The peasant was tied to
his manor and needed permission to leave it, and even the ruling class,
except when they moved in a group, had to be careful in their comings
and goings. The English had been conquered but not yet fully
subdued, and so many Normans met with nasty and fatal accidents
that a new law was found to be necessary. Any man found murdered
must be proved to be English – it was called the establishment of
Englishry; otherwise the victim would be assumed to be Norman and
punishment would fall upon the nearest English community. It was
rather difficult to make a dead Norman, even when stripped of his
clothes, look like a dead Englishman; he wore his hair differently,

shaved close around the ears and at the nape of the neck. But with enough savagery it could be done, and indeed it was done.

The people of this age were largely dependent upon their own resources for amusement. They played chess and draughts, and various games with cards and dice. Any well-born girl not stupid or tone deaf could make some sort of tune on a lute, and almost everybody could sing. Also, since the humour of the age was coarse, some fun was to be derived from the behaviour of the village idiot; even he had a role to play in the self-sufficient, tightly-knit communities of Norman England.

# 2 The Medieval Tapestry

 he Norman period lasted just under a hundred years and ended in disorder. A new line of kings coming to the throne may not appear on the surface to be a domestic affair, but it brought some small though significant changes to ordinary life. Its immediate effect was to render a number of people – all from the privileged class – homeless. Henry II, the first of the Plantagenets, intended to rule with as firm a hand as his great-grandfather the Conqueror had done, and one of the first acts of his reign was to order that all castles built without licence should be pulled down. There were more than 1100 of them, hastily and illegally erected during the civil wars between Matilda and Stephen.

The new king then set about restoring law and order and presently could claim, or have it claimed for him, that a virgin could walk, with her bosom full of gold, from end to end of his realm and not be molested. It may have been true, for he had a short way with offenders – robbers were hanged and any man who forced a woman to sexual intercourse against her will was castrated. To see that his laws were enforced he appointed judges, who made regular rounds and administered the law as it was laid down, without class distinctions or racial prejudice. The King's Law was above such things. Henry himself was of mixed blood; his grandmother was English – good Queen Maud – so his mother was half-English; his father was the Count of Anjou, but Henry had been educated in Bristol, and well-educated too. Active as he was, often not bothering to sit down to a meal, he still took delight in the company of literate and intelligent men. He was as near to cosmopolitan as a man could be at the time, and during his reign what remained of the gulf between Norman and English closed.

Even one of his taxes hints at the wind of change. He always hoped that one day, when he had everything in order, he could go on a crusade and drive the Seljuk Turks out of the Holy Land. Henry imposed a Saladin tax, named after Saladin, the leader of the infidels, to raise funds for mounting this crusade. It was the first tax in England to be levied not upon land, but upon people. It was not popular, but in its backhanded way it recognized the existence of people as people, divorced from the soil.

OPPOSITE Women carding wool. Although the woman on the right is still wearing a simple head-dress, the lady on the left has moved with the fashion.

Henry never attained his ambition to become a crusader, and the idea of crusading was left to his son, Richard, quite the most remembered crusader of them all. Brave, chivalrous, defeated on the very verge of victory, he became a legend in his lifetime. He reigned for ten years, and spent only six months in England, but he left his mark on social and therefore on domestic life.

Richard, like his father, needed money for his crusade. His method was to sell charters – the right of self-government within certain limits – to many towns. He even said he would sell London if a buyer could be found. He sold heiresses and heirs and widows, sheriffdoms in counties, and justiceships. The towns thus freed saw the beginnings of a new class – the freemen, the burgesses, a kind of middle class.

The peasant had to wait a little longer for his deliverance; but the crusade affected the countryside, too, for men were needed as well as money. It was still obligatory for a man who held his land from the king to obey the call to arms, and though Richard was willing to accept money instead of personal service he had plenty of followers. Greed was a strong motive, but the genuine feeling of piety should not be under-rated; there were countless men who were willing to face danger, privation, even death itself, in order to put Jerusalem and the rest of the Holy Land back into Christian hands.

The women stayed at home. Many of them were left to run, with the help of a steward, the whole estate. Some – young, attractive and not entirely to be trusted – were locked into that well-known contraption called a chastity belt. No man cared to be cuckolded, but men of property had a special horror of it. To think that one's possessions, one's very name, might pass to a boy sired by another man was appalling. Extra-marital relationships formed by men were far more leniently regarded; many men acknowledged their bastards and provided for them, and, in the absence of a legal heir, arranged that they should inherit.

Sterility was the worst affliction a woman could suffer in this rigidly feudal age. Rank, wealth and title all depended upon land, and land was held directly from the king in return for rendering military service. Men were reared to be fighting machines and women were regarded as breeding machines; there must be a son to inherit his father's property and obligations. Daughters were ineligible. (There are vestigial remains of this rule to this day. An English queen may wear her father's crown, but the daughter of a peer must stand aside and see the title and all that part of her father's property that is entailed pass on to the nearest male relative.) The blame for sterility, or for the bearing of girls only, was firmly laid upon the wife, though there were instances that exposed this as a fallacy. Eleanor of Aquitaine was first married to the King of France, and bore him two daughters. He managed to obtain a divorce, and Eleanor then married Henry II of England by whom she produced four great, husky, troublesome boys as well as another daughter. But the lesson implicit in this example was ignored.

This craving for sons existed at all levels; the peasant had a few animals, a few tools, his rights, his obligations and his name to pass on. When a man died, his eldest son, provided he paid the death due the lord demanded and agreed to do the labour his father had done, succeeded to the holding. Women had no rights at all and the ordinary woman spent her life in the care and protection – in fact possession – of some man. A girl's husband was chosen for her. He might be a man she had never seen, or one she had met and detested; she had no choice. In the matter of mating perhaps the peasant woman had a slight advantage; her husband could hardly be a complete stranger to her, for she could not, without the lord's permission – rarely given – marry a man from another manor. She had value as a work animal and as a potential breeder of work animals.

In the marriage market of the high-born sentiment rarely affected considerations of property, rank and political advantage though a father would look ahead and make some provision against his daughter being widowed. He would often, at the cost of some self-denial, provide his daughter with a dowry which might be matched with a marriage settlement by the prospective husband. In such warlike times it was natural for a woman to outlive her husband, but she was very fortunate if this enabled her to achieve independence. A clause in Magna Carta, 1215, stipulating that no widow should be forced into marriage by the king's order against her wishes, indicates what a frequent and resented occurrence this must have been. Another says that in case of murder a woman could not bear witness unless the murdered man was her husband. This underlines the position of women in 1215; if her husband were still alive she was an unreliable witness, forced to say what she was told to say.

The competence with which some women had administered estates and sometimes defended their absent husband's property might have done something to raise their status, but for the fact that the crusades had brought the Christian West into closer touch with the Moslem world in which women not only had few rights, but were considered to have no souls. No Christian man could quite accept *that*, but the general feeling was that, however competently a woman might act in an emergency, her real sphere was still within the home.

The home – for all but the poor – became more comfortable after the crusades. Some fortunate crusaders had looted cushions and carpets, and observant passers through Venice had seen to what use glass could be put. There were new materials, too – not only silks and velvets, but gauze, gossamer-fine, eminently suitable for head-dresses (it took its name from Gaza); and there was a new kind of silk cloth called bauldekin, said to come from Babylon, a place about which few people had ever heard.

Some crusaders brought plants, little cuttings, seeds, or bulbs. How many dwindled and died we cannot know; the snowdrop certainly

In medieval times the towns really started to develop. The church is the dominant feature in this walled and fortified town, and the dancing people suggest that a festival is being celebrated.

flourished so well that it is usually regarded as indigenous. The owners of some old cedar trees claim that they are now 900 years old, and it is pleasant, if romantic, to visualize some crusader, impressed by the massive dignity of the tree, tucking a fertile cone into his baggage.

Contact with the East had other effects, too; Arabic numerals were adopted, which must have greatly simplified arithmetic. The Arab horse, lighter and fleeter than its European counterpart, was introduced. Eastern medical knowledge was found to be ahead of that in the West. Men had tasted the wine of Crete and found it to their liking; and they had seen lamps fuelled with olive oil.

The period after the crusades saw a great expansion of trade which particularly benefited the freemen of the towns. There were nearly 200 cities and boroughs in England by the end of the thirteenth century, but they were still very small: Cambridge, for example, had only 550 households and Manchester 150. But although the towns represented a small part of the population their military and trading importance was very great and they nurtured the development of an independent middle class which broke up the rigid feudal division between the labourer and the landowner. To check the aspirations of this new class laws were repeatedly passed restricting the use of certain materials and furs to people of certain rank. In 1285 the *City Letter Book Regulations* declared:

> . . . no woman of the City shall from henceforth go to market, or in the King's highway, out of her house, with a hood furred with other than lambskin or rabbitskin, on pain of losing her hood to the use of the Sheriffs. . . . And this because that regratresses [retailers], nurses and other servants, and women of loose life, bedizen themselves, and wear hoods furred with gros vair and with miniver, in guise of good ladies.

The fact that such rules had to be repeated again and again proves that they were ineffectual. To order a woman who could afford miniver and silk to wear only cony and woollen cloth was to spit against the wind.

The position of women definitely improved within this middle class; it was possible for them to become unofficial but important partners in their husbands' enterprises, or even to operate minor businesses, such as alehouses, cookshops and bakehouses, on their own. Chaucer's description of the Wife of Bath in *The Canterbury Tales* gives a

Although the crusaders had discovered the oil lamp on their travels, candles, sometimes in very beautiful candlesticks, continued to be in common use for a long time.

delightful picture of how independent a townswoman could have
become in the late fourteenth century. The Wife of Bath had enjoyed
five husbands as well as 'oother companye in youthe'; she had
travelled on several pilgrimages; her clothmaking surpassed that of
Ypres and Ghent and she was gaily dressed:

> Hir coverchiefs ful fyne were of ground;
> I dorste swere they weyeden ten pound,
> That on a Sunday were upon hir heed.
> Hir hosen weren of fyn scarlet reed
> Full streite y-teyd, and shoes ful moyste and newe;
> Boold was hir face and fair and reed of hewe.

As citizens became more prosperous it was possible to use more stone
and brick for domestic building. This was encouraged by the authorities because of the ever-present risk of fire, vividly described in *The
White Book of the City of London* compiled in 1419.

It should be remarked that in ancient times the greater part of the City was
built of wood, and the houses were covered with straw, stubble and the like.

Hence it happened, that when a single house had caught fire, the greater
part of the City was destroyed through such conflagration; a thing that took
place in the first year of the reign of King Stephen, when, by reason of a fire
that broke out at London Bridge, the church of Saint Paul was burnt; from
which spot the conflagration extended, destroying houses and buildings, as
far as the church of St Clement Danes.

After this, many of the citizens, to avoid such a peril, built stone houses
upon their foundations covered with thick tiles, and so protected against
the fury of the flames; whence it has often been the case that, when a fire has
broken out in the city, and has destroyed many buildings, upon reaching
such houses, it has been unable to do further mischief, and has been
extinguished; so that, through such a house as this the houses of the
neighbours have been saved from being burnt.

Nevertheless, despite this encouraging development, so many wooden
buildings remained that fire was a continuing threat to the town-
dweller for centuries to come.

Sanitation was another hazard of the crowded communities. Some
houses had privies which emptied into a ditch or river, but all too often

Chaucer's well-dressed Wife of Bath – an independent, emancipated woman by the standards of the times.

In this period masons and carpenters were rarely short of work. Some of their tools and methods are still in common use today – the man at the top left, for instance, is using a plumbline, while the man below him is hauling up materials using a windlass and bucket.

a housewife or servant on an upper floor found it easier to empty the brimming chamber pot out of the window, warning passers-by with a shout of 'gardy-loo' (*gardez l'eau*, beware of the water). Town authorities made repeated efforts to deal with the filthy streets, employing 'rakyers' to remove the rubbish and passing a host of ineffectual ordinances such as 'That no one shall throw dung into the King's highway or before the house of his neighbour'; 'That each person shall make clean of filth the front of his house under penalty of half a mark.'

Every town had an open sewer called the town ditch, which was required to deal with what the butchers in the shambles flung out; with the overflow of tanpits where hides were made into leather; and with what came from the places where linen was retted – a stinking process. Rules about what might not be thrown into the town ditch were regularly made, and as regularly evaded. But with one good sharp shower, or the cumulative effect of a few days of steady, gentler rain, the town ditch was cleansed, emptying itself into the nearest stream, which would eventually flow into a river and so into the sea. Even London could not yet pollute the Thames to the point where the salmon were discouraged. Streams like the Fleet River and Walbrook, flowing less vigorously, and often with latrines built over them, did sometimes become clogged and offensive enough to warrant complaint. Clearing operations were then undertaken, and new laws passed and disobeyed. There was no real improvement. Even when such streams and some town ditches were roofed over, thus mitigating the affront to eye and nose, their real condition remained unchanged and the hazard to health remained.

In the sparsely populated countryside sanitation was less of a problem. For the cottager the matter was simple. The value of manure was recognized. (Some tenants and landlords had disputes about where various animals should be penned for the night, in other words whose land should benefit from the dung dropped.) Close by every dwelling there was a midden, or manure heap. Indeed some people believe that the site of a long vanished house can be determined by the presence of a good crop of nettles growing on the place where the midden once was. The peasant and his family simply went out and contributed. It was unpleasant in cold weather for everyone, and awkward for the old or infirm, so ingenious men built little shelters, with a raised seat over a hole – the outside privy, or necessary house, which served houses of some grandeur until the end of the nineteenth century, humbler homes for many years after that, and is still to be seen in remote places.

Castles, however, enjoyed a very early form of indoor sanitation; apartments known as garde-robes. The name came from their secondary purpose – the preservation of furs and heavy woollen clothes from the ravages of moth during the summer. The garde-robe usually occupied a corner position, or even a projecting tower, and the well designed castle had one on each floor. The seat was sometimes made of wood, though more often of stone, and the sewage simply fell, occasionally into a kind of chute, but more usually down the wall of the castle itself, leaving an unsightly, slimy trail which ended in the moat or on the mound upon which the castle stood. It is not unlikely that buckets of water were emptied through the same hole now and again. Winter clothes hung on the walls and it has been suggested that it was the draught which deterred the moths. However, since the medieval castle had no lack of draughty places it is more likely that the ammoniac stench kept the moths away.

Curiously, although our ancestors did make some connection between evil odours and ill health, they appear to have been blind to the real risk which was that of drinking water contaminated by sewage. Water was dipped from the nearest stream, or fetched from the nearest well. The wonder is not that disease was prevalent, but that there was not more of it. The stark truth was that those people who had survived the ills of childhood had developed sturdy constitutions and acquired a certain immunity.

With typical insularity, people believed that the real pestilence – a vague, over-all term – came in from abroad, carried by people who travelled, or borne on the wind from the south. The belief in airborne infection persisted well on into Tudor times when many new houses were built; other factors being equal, the south-facing aspect was avoided. Native illnesses abounded, some of them caused by the climate – the other side of the coin which so often prevented epidemics. Innumerable children died of croup. Bronchitis could strike young and old alike, and rheumatism, sometimes called the joint evil, was the almost invariable accompaniment of advancing age, especially among people who worked out of doors in all weathers and lived in cottages with damp earthen floors.

The woman of the house was supposed to be both physician and pharmacist. At all levels medical lore was handed down from older women to the younger ones. Doctors lived only in towns, were remarkably high-handed and made preposterous charges. Surgeons were a despised race, amateurs who pursued other trades such as those of butcher, blacksmith and barber. But humble though they were,

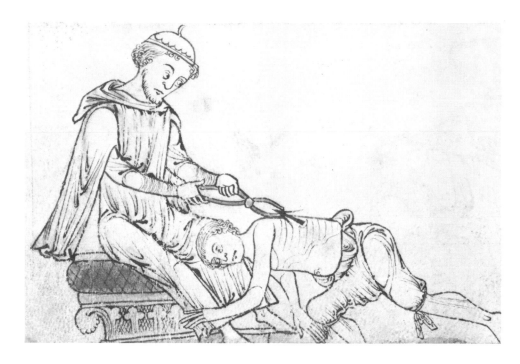

Medieval medicine, fortunately, has changed. A doctor uses pliers to remove an arrow from his patient's back.

they were often, through experience, more effective in their own field than the physicians were in theirs. They learned by watching and doing, yet because they had no claim to scholarship they remained unrecognized. In the late fourteenth century Johannes de Mirfield described how:

... ignorant amateurs, to say nothing of – what is worse and is considered by me more horrible – worthless and presumptuous women, usurp this profession to themselves and abuse it; who possessing neither natural ability nor professional knowledge, make the greatest possible mistakes (thanks to their stupidity) and very often kill their patients. . . .

However, it seems unlikely that Johannes de Mirfield was any better than the amateurs he scorned, for he also wrote:

Take the name of the patient, the name of the messenger sent to summon the physician, and the name of the day upon which the messenger first came to you; join all their letters together and if an even number result, the patient will not escape; if the number be odd, then he will recover.

The well-to-do could afford opium for the relief of pain, and a clove for an aching tooth, but the poor depended upon native plants, the wild things available to anyone who knew what to look for, and how to use it. Books about herbs came later in time, and some of them made extraordinary claims, but some herbs survived the test of time. Horehound – the white variety, bruised, boiled to a thin syrup and mixed with honey – was used long before it was written about; it cured coughs in Norman England and was an ingredient of cough mixtures sold 900 years later. (The efficacy of the other horehound, called black or stinking, may have been psychological; infused it was a cure for hysterics. Nobody could face a second dose.) Foxglove, stems, flowers or leaves, made into an infusion, spurred on the flagging, tired heart – and continued to do so until digitalis was synthetically produced. And pennyroyal held its own as an abortifacient well into the twentieth century.

Ointments were also required. For most of them goosegrease, in itself an emollient, formed a good base, but it was slippery stuff and worked better when made a little firmer by the addition of mutton fat or beeswax. It was good for chilblains and other kinds of sore, and, taken by mouth, eased hoarseness. Mixed with resin from any coniferous tree it also made a liniment which, well rubbed in, eased the pain of strained joints and stiff muscles.

The country people did their best with what they had, knew or believed, and alongside the myths – such as a fried mouse being a cure for whooping cough – was one apparently superstitious habit now known to be based upon scientific fact. Smallpox was greatly dreaded because of its after-effects. Other pestilences, if survived, could be forgotten; smallpox often left the survivor hideously disfigured. Such a state was more tragic for women than for men, but it was so common that a face even lightly scarred was considered beautiful. It was customary, in households which could afford it, to wrap the smallpox victim in red flannel, and to cover the window with red cloth. This did not cure the disease or stave off death, but the survivor thus treated emerged less badly pitted than one for whom no such precaution had been taken. Later generations dismissed this as mere superstition. Fairly recently it has been established that the occlusion of certain light rays promotes healing without scarring, and that one way of treating the light is to pass it through a red screen.

The gay and spectacular medieval clothes which brighten the pages of illuminated manuscripts seem to have appeared, at court at least, by the death of William Rufus in 1100, for William of Malmesbury writes of his reign: 'Then was there flowing hair and extravagant dress; and then was invented the fashion of shoes curved with points; then the model of young men was to rival women in delicacy of person, to mince their gait. . . .' Men's fashions became more extravagant as the Middle Ages passed, until toe points were so long that they were chained to the waist and sleeves had to be knotted before the wearer could eat. By the late fourteenth century young men had rejected the traditional long gown in favour of a short jacket with tight-fitting 'hosen', sometimes with legs of different colours. For older men the long gown remained in fashion until Tudor times, but it was made of the richest material in lavish quantities.

Obviously ordinary people could not afford such clothes, but as we have already seen they were so ready to ape their betters that laws had to be passed to restrain them. Even the clothes of peasants were regulated by law, as in a statute of 1363 that 'all manner of people . . . attendying to husbandry and al maner of people, that hath not 40s of goods nor of cattals shall not take nor weare no maner of clothe but blanket and russet wolle of 12d and shall wear the gyrdels of linnen accordynge to their estate.'

For women the clothes were pretty, if in some cases painful. Every woman must now have a waist, sharply defined and the smaller the better. Those denied such a thing by nature did the best they could with fierce corsets of stout linen reinforced by stiff leather, or even iron. Necklines dropped. Hair – so long hidden – was displayed, elaborately dressed and if necessary supplemented by hair grown on another head or puffed out over pads of wool. Skirts were provocatively slit from knee to ankle. Most spectacular of all were the head-dresses, whose only purpose was to be charming, a far cry from the old nun-like article. Some were in the form of a pair of horns, some were steeple-shaped, and the prettiest of all were like butterflies. Such fashions

The medieval table had acquired some sophistication over its Norman counterpart – knives are used (though not forks for some time). The vessels are elegant, but even at a royal feast trencher bread and roughly jointed meats are much in evidence. The younger men wear short tunics with hose, while the older ones wear long gowns. Practically all of them are sporting the very long pointed shoes that were so fashionable then.

Sir Geoffrey Luttrell bids farewell to his wife and daughter-in-law, who holds out his shield for him. Note the narrow bodices and flowing hems of the mid-fourteenth-century dresses in this illustration from the Luttrell Psalter.

horrified churchmen who denounced them from the pulpit and drew cartoons showing the devil lacing himself into a tight gown, draping his real horns with gauze, or riding merrily on a lady's train. Nobody took any notice.

Sadly, too many memorial brasses have been ripped up, but some of the remaining ones show how charming the new fashions were, the narrow waists emphasized by the spreading head-dresses and the fullness of the skirts at the hem. When a number of women in such clothes gathered, perhaps to watch a tournament from the ladies' gallery at the side of the tourney ground, they must have looked like a flower garden. Scent was popular, too. The fastidious woman had always laid her clothes away in chests with sweet-smelling herbs – lavender, rosemary, southernwood. Trade with the East had brought heavier, headier perfumes, some of them of animal origin, derived from the civet cat and the musk deer. Since these scents were produced by the animals for the purpose of sexual attraction it was only a small step to consider that they had aphrodisiac qualities; and much later in history, when prudery was in vogue, no self-respecting woman would allow herself anything more than a dash of lavender water or eau de cologne. To indulge in anything else was to smell like a tart.

In the Middle Ages sweet odours were certainly desirable; there were far too many of the other kind. They were caused not only by the lack of sewers and drains, but by bodies seldom or never completely washed. The habit of regular bathing had gone out with the Romans. The early fathers of the Church are said to have disapproved of bathing because the Roman public baths, which allowed mixed bathing, had been centres of licentiousness. Certainly some of the early saints, squatting on top of pillars for years on end, or dwelling in narrow caves, could not have set high store on cleanliness.

Sometime in the reign of Richard II in the late fourteenth century the Mayor of London did set up public bath-houses, but they soon fell into disrepute. The dainty-looking medieval lady would, if she were

A medieval lady taking a rare bath, watched eagerly by a knight who appears somewhat absent-mindedly to have brought his horse in with him.

fastidious, take a bath occasionally in her own home, using a half cask.

The idle fashions of the medieval period should not disguise the fact that the main pursuit of the upper classes was still warfare and that pointed shoes were frequently discarded for suits of armour. Edward II, Richard II, Henry VI and Richard III all lost their thrones in civil war, while strong kings like Edward I and Henry V expended their energies against the Scots, Welsh or French. The domestic development of England therefore took place against a background of intermittent fighting.

But the most severe damage to the nation came from an unseen, undefeatable enemy which had set out from China and been on the move for twenty years – the Black Death. It reached England at the end of 1348 and did its worst the following year. England had always had plagues and pestilences, if not epidemic, then endemic, just around the corner, but never anything like this. In the absence of official records, the damage is difficult to estimate; what few records do

Medieval England was frequently in the grip of both foreign and civil wars, and men of the upper classes would certainly have spent long periods away from their families and estates. Under the chain mail a kind of loose shirt was worn.

exist hint that a death rate of fifty per cent of the population is no exaggeration. The Goldsmiths' Company in London, which normally elected a Master to head it for a year, had four in 1349; in Bristol the living were too few to bury the dead. The filthy crowded towns suffered worse, but it ravaged the countryside too. In Kent the chronicler William of Dene, a Rochester monk, recorded:

In this year a plague of a kind which had never been met with before ravaged our land of England. The Bishop of Rochester, who maintained only a small household, lost four priests, five esquires, ten attendants, seven young clerics and six pages, so that nobody was left to serve him in any capacity. . . .

To our great grief the plague carried off so vast a multitude of people of both sexes that nobody could be found who would bear the corpses to the grave. Men and women carried their own children on their shoulders to the church and threw them into a common pit.

East Anglia and Yorkshire suffered so badly that whole villages were wiped out, and land long cultivated went back to the waste. Some country churches keep a record of priests-in-charge, and four or five changes in a year testify to the stout-heartedness of the priests and the deadliness of the plague. In the end there was no one to administer the last rites or conduct funeral services. Animals, untended, died, and their carcasses rotted, adding to the general horror. (It is still possible in one part of Suffolk to drive for several miles between well-cultivated fields and see no big house, no cottage, and to feel an unaccountable sense of desolation as well as to wonder who works the land. A closer examination of the history of the Black Death reveals that it was a particularly devastated area, and when the land was brought back into cultivation it was tilled by people who already had established homes in a less hard-hit village, some distance away.)

Those who survived lived on in a changed world. The old feudal system had been shaken. The Black Death had been no respecter of persons – lords and ladies had died too – and a man who had possessed one manor found himself responsible for two or three with a sorely depleted labour force to work them. The ploughmen suddenly realized their worth and demanded wages. The serf was no longer a serf; he was a man with something to sell – his hands, his knowledge. 'There was so marked a deficiency of labourers and workmen of every kind at this

The Dalynrugge
Brass from Fletching
Church, Sussex,
shows a knight in full
armour with a lion
crouched at his feet,
while his lady is
depicted with her pet
dog.

period,' wrote William of Dene, 'that more than a third of the land in the whole realm was let idle. All the labourers skilled, or unskilled, were so carried away by the spirit of revolt that neither King, nor law, nor justice, could restrain them. . . .' Reactionary laws were passed; wages were fixed; a serf who left his manor to work on another where the pay was better must be returned and branded. It was useless. There was little *esprit de corps* between landowners, anxious to avert the threatened famine. Famine was very close in 1349–50; near enough – together with a shortage of men – to halt the Hundred Years ·War with France for seven years.

When the law failed to restore the manorial system, sensible landowners sought other solutions. One was to put land down to sheep – a man and a dog could tend sheep over an area that had taken twenty men to plough and seed and reap. Another was to sell or rent land to the man who wanted to be independent. Most men did; they were certain that with their own hands, and those of their wives and children, they could make a living, pay their rent in money, and release themselves from servitude. The age of the freeman, the yeoman of England – long the envy of other countries – had begun, and the revolution for which France must wait until 1789 and Russia until 1917 had come about, without bloodshed.

The farm wife pulled her weight in making the new system work. She still helped in the field, especially during haymaking and at the harvest, but in an economy where money had become important, she needed something to sell; she found it in the dairy, in the yard where the poultry ran. To this period belongs the traditional farm wife plodding to market with panniers of produce on a horse or donkey. It was customary until the middle of this century, when factory farming began its hideous rule, for the wife of a small farmer to have her own egg and butter money, to spend as she liked.

The farm wife's other reward was improved living accommodation. She would naturally need a dairy, facing north for coolness, and at least one slate shelf on which butter could be worked. The milk was poured into shallow, wide-mouthed crocks so that the cream could rise and be skimmed off with an implement resembling a plate with holes in it, so that any milk dipped up could drip back. The cream was then put into a taller, narrower crock and left to ripen – the exact stage in the process being a matter for experience to gauge. Then it was churned in small tubs in which the cream was agitated by a paddle with four blades.

Butter was sold by the pint, and its importance as a commodity is recalled by place names in old towns – Butter Market, Butter Cross. By some happy chance supply and demand coincided. In earlier times butter had not been regarded as part of the ordinary diet; it was used for cooking and as a medicine; it cured constipation and was very good for puny children. Now it came to table in the 'lordly dish' mentioned in the Bible. The quality varied according to the care and skill that went into its making and the good buttermakers sold out first. The buttermilk left in the churn made a cool, pleasantly near-sour drink for humans, and played a good part in the feeding of pigs; and in times of plenty butter could be salted down for use in winter.

Cheese often went to market alongside the butter. Cheeses were not yet distinguished by name but fell into two classes, soft and hard. The soft were made from cream, or from milk with cream added, and they were intended for immediate consumption. Hard cheese, properly made and stored in a cool airy place, would keep for a long time. For making cheese the milk had to be sour, and the process could be speeded by adding some curdling agent. The best known one is rennet, but on a medieval farm this must have been in short supply since it came from the stomach of a calf, and few calves or other immature animals were killed in those days when the young must be coddled along until they had acquired some weight. Poorer people regarded the eating of any young beast as reckless extravagance. Even among the rich who could afford it, veal was not popular, since on its own it lacked taste and needed added flavourings to make it palatable. It was known as froth meat. A rhyme was even made up about it; he who ate *froth* might soon lack *broth*.

Substitutes for rennet were well known; the juice of the wild sorrel was one. When the curd had set it was broken up, by hand – calamitous to the fingernails – or sliced and re-sliced with a knife. It was then cooked, very slowly, for about two hours, strained in a cloth and pressed. The fortunate farmwife had a cheese press, similar to those

OPPOSITE A woman milking a cow, from an early English illuminated manuscript.

Acca dicta qi boacca. Est enim ex qu

used for pressing linen or in bookbinding except that its slabs were often made of stone. When the last drop of moisture had been extracted, the cheeses were moulded by hand, wrapped in dry cloths and set on a high, airy shelf to dry; they were turned at regular intervals, so that the protective rind might form evenly. A good deal of cheese was reserved for family use, since it kept well, was portable, and was sustaining. Nobody knew then that the Roman legions had marched on a staple diet of bread and cheese; but they did know that people could perform hard manual work on such food, with, perhaps, an onion for flavour.

Another 'mod con' which the woman of this emerging class wanted, and often attained, was a proper oven. It is still possible to see a brick chimney breast built outside, but attached to, the gable end of an old house. This enabled the woman on the inner side of the wall to have her side hearth – the famous kitchen fire – and her oven. This kind of outside structure can help to date a house. In Tudor buildings the chimney tended to be an integral part of the structure.

Improvements to old houses, and the building of new ones, could be afforded by those who produced anything marketable, and the newly independent farmers were great producers. The size and even the shape of their holdings varied. In some villages the open field system survived; a few survived even the Tudor enclosures and were dispensed with only in the eighteenth century. But it was plain that the man on his own did better with his bit of enclosed land where he was not the victim of a neighbour's carelessness about such things as weeds, or a sick animal infecting healthy ones. Experts can now ascertain, by an analysis of the plants, shrubs and trees that make up a hedgerow, how old it is; and some are very old indeed.

The goose deserves a mention, for it contributed to this prosperity. They were not the easiest of birds to rear: they mated for life so that a gander deprived of his goose, or a goose of her gander, pined and was good for nothing but the pot; they were not egg layers; and they were vegetarian, eating only grass, so that when the pasture died down in autumn the birds must be fed. But the goose was a valuable bird – apart from its edibility, the down from its breast made the softest pillows, and its wing feathers made quills for writing.

OPPOSITE An aristocratic riding party in the late Middle Ages. Note the richness of the clothing of both sexes, and the two-horned head-dresses worn by the women.

A goose for Michaelmas, when grass began to get scarce, was a popular dish. A few lived longer, being fattened for Christmas; though not quite in the cruel Strasbourg style, the aim being not an over-large liver, but a nice fat bird. Some travelled, on foot, to London and other hungry towns. Their feet were given a protective covering of tar and they were herded along by trusted women – agents really – who knew the way, and the market.

Much of what the farmer's wife had to sell was bought by her town counterpart, the tradesman's wife, sensible enough to do her own marketing – who else could be trusted to be discriminating, or to do a bit of haggling? A maidservant, or, surer sign of status, a boy, walked behind his mistress carrying baskets, presently to be laden. Part affectation, but part necessity too; for the town wife often had to buy not only for her family but for a horde of ever-hungry apprentices.

The guilds, which had begun as friendly societies – poor men gathering together for mutual aid in hard times – had become what were virtually closed shop unions. Even in the new, relatively free society, nobody could suddenly say 'I will be a blacksmith (or a carpenter or a mason).' Anyone aspiring to such a craft had first to serve an apprenticeship, drawn up in formal terms with obligations on both sides and penalties if the rules were ignored. Often a premium was paid and the apprentice usually became part of the household, so that the master could see to it that the boy learned and behaved himself, and the mistress of the household took care of his physical welfare. In *The Cook's Tale* Chaucer describes a very jolly apprentice who, despite being chided 'bothe erly and late' did not take his duties seriously.

> He loved bet the tavern than the shoppe.
> For when ther any ryding was in Chepe,
> Out of the shoppe thider wolde he lepe.
> Til that he hadde the sighte y-seyn,
> And danced wel, he wolde nat come ageyn.

But such behaviour was not tolerated for long, and the apprentice was in the end dismissed.

Sending children away from home for training was also a feature of

He that giueth meafure,
God bleffe the with treafure.

It makes a poore man,
To fell flower for bran.

God bleffeth trewe labour,
with plentye and fauour.

Looke well to thy feafon,
with cunninge and reafon.

Be iuft with thy weightes,
God plague falfe fleights.

Pricke not at thy pleafure,
But in trewe houfhold meafure.

Who fo followeth their preceptes well,

In heauen fhall haue a place to dwell

An enormous number of trades and crafts were practised in the largely self-supporting medieval town.

FAR LEFT Scenes of activity in a bakery, from the manual of the Bakers' Company of the City of York.

LEFT A clockmaker in his workshop. The man in the foreground is doing sums on an abacus.

FAR LEFT Haggling at market stalls.

LEFT The delightful memorial brass of a medieval glover.

upper-class life as a shocked Italian visitor makes clear in his *Relation* written at the end of the fifteenth century.

> The want of affection in the English is straightly manifested towards their children; for after having kept them at home till they arrive at the age of 7 or 9 years at the utmost, they put them out, both males and females, to hard service in the houses of other people, binding them generally for another 7 or 9 years. And these are called apprentices; and few are born who are exempted from this fate, for everyone, however rich he be, sends away his children into the houses of others, whilst he, in return, receives those of strangers into his own.

The reason the English gave for this, said the author, was that the children learnt better manners but he attributed it to purely selfish motives: '... they are better served by strangers than they would be by their own children.' (The popularity of the English boarding school therefore has a long history of tradition behind it. It is interesting that the habit of sending children from home at a very tender age is far less prevalent in America where there is no feudal tradition.)

The emphasis on 'courtesy' in medieval romances shows how important manners were in upper-class life. *The Babees' Book* was specially written for young princes around 1475, and gives a bewildering array of instructions to the young, for example:

> When you enter your lord's place say 'Good speed', and with humble cheer greet all who are there present. Do not rush in rudely, but enter with head up and at an easy pace, and kneel on one knee only to your lord or sovereign.
>
> Take no seat, but be ready to stand until you are bidden to sit down. Keep your hands and feet at rest; do not claw your flesh or lean against a post, in the presence of your lord, or handle anything belonging to the house.

Table manners are minutely described in *The Babees' Book* and many of its rules survive to the present day:

> Look ye be not caught leaning on the table, and keep clear of soiling the cloth.
>
> Do not carry your knife to your mouth with food, or hold the meat with your hands in any wise.
>
> Do not cut your meat like field-men who have such an appetite that they reck not in what wise, where or when or how ungoodly they hack at their

In the days when cane sugar was not yet imported, and long before sugar beet was grown as a crop, honey was the only sweetening agent known and bees were widely kept.

meat; but, sweet children, have always your delight in courtesy and in gentleness and eschew boisterousness with all your might.

Girls were sent away not only to learn manners but in the hope of making a good marriage. Thus prudent parents always tried to send their daughters to a household just a shade superior in social status to their own. A girl who failed to marry was often sent to a nunnery; even here a dowry was necessary before her acceptance.

The tales of romantic and courtly love which were so popular in

A kind of early ball game for the ordinary people. . .

medieval times encouraged a more emotional approach to the choice of marriage partners, but even at the end of the Middle Ages a love match was still exceptional. *The Paston Letters*, written in the fifteenth century by members of a well-to-do landowning family, illustrate this all too well. When Elizabeth Paston was reluctant to marry a widower of fifty she was 'beaten once in the week or twice, sometimes twice in one day, and her head broken in two or three places'. This treatment continued for nearly three months! Another Paston, Margery, secretly plighted herself to the bailiff of the Paston estates. This outraged her family: 'He should never have my goodwill for to make my sister to sell candle and mustard in Framlingham', wrote a brother. For years pressure was put on Margery to revoke the betrothal and when the family at last allowed the marriage to proceed, her husband was never admitted to the family circle and Margery was left nothing in her mother's will. The only happy Paston love story involved John Paston and Margery Brews in 1477. The love match nearly faltered on the question of dowry and Margery wrote apologetically to her lover: 'My lady my mother has laboured the matter to my father full diligently but she can no more get than ye know of, for the which God knoweth I am full sorry. But if that ye love me, as I trust verily that ye do, ye will not leave me therefore.' Happily John could not resist such a plea and

made her 'the merriest maiden on ground' by accepting the dowry, small though it was.

The amusements of the upper class remained chiefly hunting, hawking, tournaments and feasting. There was a growing interest in literature especially after the fourteenth century when the English language first flowered into verse under Chaucer's hand, but books were still copied by scribes and even the rich could not afford many. Caxton's printing press was not set up in Westminster until 1476, on the verge of the Tudor period.

The common people of course had much less opportunity for leisure but there were numerous church feast days on which no work was done and which were often celebrated with fairs, or miracle plays or particular traditions. On the feast of the nativity of St John, for example, people stayed at home and 'made three maner of fire: one was clene bones and noo woode, and that is called a Bone Fyre . . . another is clene woode, and no bones, and that is called a Wode Fyre . . . the thirde is made of wode and bones, and it is called Saynt Johannes fyre.' The bone fire was supposed to keep dragons away; the wood fire was for brightness, showing that St John 'was a lanterne of lyght to the people' and the third fire symbolized St John's martyrdom 'for hys bones were brente'.

. . . and stag-hunting for the rich.

This illuminated capital depicts a medieval midwife with a mother and baby.

The happiest secular day in the year was the first of May when branches of trees and flowers were gathered in the woods and the village folk danced around the maypole. Their relief at the coming of spring, with its promise of warmth and light and fresh food, can easily be understood. An anonymous fifteenth century poem expresses the joy of a May morning:

> In somer when the shawes be sheyne
>> And leves be large and long
> Hit is full merry in feyre foreste
>> To hear the foulys song.
>
> To see the dere draw to the dale
>> And leve the hilles hee,
> And shadow him on the leves grene
>> Under the green-wode tree.
>
> Hit befell on Whitsontide
>> Early in a May mornyng,
> The Sunne up faire can shyne
>> And the briddis mery can syng
>
> This is a mery mornynge' said Litulle Johne
>> 'Be Hym that dyed on tre;
> A more mery man than I am one
>> Lyves not in Christiante.'

The medieval fairs began as annual markets serving a wider area than the weekly ones, but wherever people gathered in numbers and money was on the move, less serious activities were bound to be attracted. A crowd must be offered refreshment and amusement. Many of the entertainments were brutal but it was not a squeamish age; most people, even the ladies, enjoyed the bull or bear baiting, the dog and cock fights, a good bout of fisticuffs or the sight of two sturdy fellows, armed with clubs, taking cracks at each other's shins. Most fairs were timed to take place when the harvest was in, and before the bad weather arrived. However St Bartholomew's, a famous London fair, was held in August, perhaps because London was even then sufficiently urbanized as to have lost regard for the routine of the country year. The Oxford Fair, named after St Giles, was held early in

A farmer taking an apparently reluctant beast to market.

September, and the famous Stourbridge Fair, just outside Cambridge, began on 18 September and lasted eleven days. The Ely Fair, St Audrey's, gave a new word to the language, *tawdry*, meaning an inferior if superficially attractive thing. Most people who attended the fair knew somebody left at home who was wanting a 'fairing', who would be pleased by its appearance, and not over-critical as to its lasting value.

Below the noise and the glitter a great deal of serious business was done; the fairs were sufficiently important to attract buyers and sellers from overseas. Most of the tar, so essential to the sheep farmer and the goose breeder, came in from the Baltic by way of the fairs, and the foreigners went home with English woollen cloth and hides. Fairs held in early autumn also served as labour exchanges. Michaelmas was not far distant and men and women whose contract with their present employer ended on that Quarter Day, and who wished for change, could attend a fair and offer their services. They had no need to speak;

they merely carried something indicative of their craft – a shepherd a crook or a wisp of wool, a maid a mop.

That within a relatively short time of the acute labour shortage that followed the Black Death in 1348–9 men and women should be offering themselves for hire is an indication of how the population had recovered and how the new, freer, more mobile society had not brought equal benefit to all. The strong, the energetic and the fortunate, both in town and country, had benefited enormously from the breakdown of the rigid system; those less adequate had suffered a decline in fortune and drifted on to the free labour market, so much more competitive than the old manorial system, when everything was ordered from above and obedience was more valued than enterprise. Pleasant though it would be to leave the Middle Ages in the merriment of the fair it must be remembered that for a large number of the population life was still a cold, hungry and exhausting business. Langland gives a touching description of the poor in *The Vision of Piers Plowman* written in the last quarter of the fourteenth century, after the Black Death had brought some improvement to the common lot.

> The needy are our neighbours, if we note rightly;
> As prisoners in cells, or poor folk in hovels,
> Charged with children and overcharged by landlords,
> What they may spare in spinning they spend on rental,
> On milk or on meal to make porridge
> To still the sobbing children at meal time.
> Also they themselves suffer much hunger.
> They have woe in wintertime, and wake at mid-night
> To rise and rock the cradle at the bedside,
> To card and to comb, to darn clouts and wash them
> To rub and to reel and put rushes on the paving.
> The woe of these women who dwell in hovels
> Is too sad to speak of or to say in rhyme.

# 3 Merrie England

In 1485 Henry Tudor defeated Richard III at the battle of Bosworth and established a new and famous dynasty of monarchs. But although his battle did mark a great milestone in history it should not be thought that the Middle Ages disappeared overnight. The Renaissance movement was already astir in Europe and the Reformation was only a few years ahead, yet the life of the people carried on much the same in Henry VII's reign as it had for a century before. Great changes were afoot but their influence on the domestic scene was very gradual.

The chief blessing which Henry VII conferred on the nation was peace and order after the intermittent warfare of the Wars of the Roses which had ended at Bosworth. The new stability of the kingdom encouraged a trend which had been developing in the fifteenth century – to build for domestic comfort and not for military security. Many of the builders were the 'new men' who had risen from the middle classes or below to be lawyers or crown servants. They made their fortunes in their chosen sphere and built a mansion to prove they had arrived, or to house the new dynasty they hoped to found. Wolsey, the most famous of all, was the son of a butcher and grazier; his successor Thomas Cromwell had a very versatile father, in turn blacksmith, brewer and innkeeper. Even the famous Bacon family had a shepherd among their forbears.

The ladder by which they climbed was education, as Bishop Latimer made clear in the first sermon he preached to Edward VI, in which he pleaded the cause of the yeoman class from which he had sprung.

> My father was a yeoman and had no lands of his own, only he had a farm of three or four pound by year at the uttermost, and hereupon he tilled so much as kept half-a-dozen men. He had walk for a hundred sheep, and my mother milked thirty kine. . . . He kept me to school or else I had not been able to have preached before the king's majesty now.

It was a tribute to medieval benefactors, churches, towns and guilds that there was so much free schooling available. Great schools like Winchester and Eton had been founded for 'poor and needy scholars' and most large towns had their own grammar school or cathedral

OPPOSITE Edward VI's coronation procession gives a good idea of what London looked like in Tudor times. It was still little more than a compact town with small, wooden, gabled houses closely huddled together, and green fields never far away. The artist of this charming picture had little idea of perspective or proportion, and some of his figures are as large as the houses they have come out of!

school. If a family could but afford to feed and clothe a boy through school and university he had a promising future. The result was that the real administration of England passed into the hands of able and astute men; what remained of the old aristocracy could become courtiers or expect command of any military or naval enterprise.

Since the new men were anxious to make their mark, many Tudor buildings were characterized by ostenation as well as comfort. Wolsey over-reached himself at Hampton Court and Henry VIII's envy was so great that, when out of favour, Wolsey deemed it a politic move to offer it to Henry as a gift. Robert Cecil suffered a similar fate at Theobalds which his father had built for the Cecil family; James I took such a fancy to the house that he asked Robert to exchange it for the old palace at Hatfield. The splendid Jacobean mansion Hatfield House was the result, and the later building contrasts strikingly with the comparatively humble Old Hall which had been grand enough for kings and bishops in an earlier era.

In the great Tudor and Jacobean houses the hall was still the heart of the house. It often extended to the roof and had a gallery built out at bedroom level for the accommodation of minstrels and players. It was furnished now with very solid tables, backed and padded benches, iron stands which could hold a number of candles, with the old open cupboards for the display of silverware, and the simpler side-table or buffet from which food could be served. Richly carved screens stood between hall and kitchen. Rushes were still spread as a floor covering; even the great Wolsey still used them – but he did use a kind which gave out a sweet scent when trodden upon. When he fell from power and no charge was too extreme or too trivial to be held against him, one charge was of extravagance; he had brought these rushes from a considerable distance, at vast expense.

An Italian visitor to Britain in the reign of Henry VII described the use of rushes in a letter he sent home:

All the streets are so badly paved that they get wet at the slightest quantity of water and this happens very frequently owing to the large numbers of cattle carrying water as well as on account of the rain, of which there is a great deal in this island. Then a vast amount of evil-smelling mud is formed. . . . The citizens, therefore, in order to remove this mud and filfth

OPPOSITE ABOVE
*Marriage Fête at Bermondsey*, painted by J. Hoefnagel. Bermondsey, now in the heart of the East End of London, was a small countrified village in Tudor times. The thatched, half-timbered houses are typical of the period.

OPPOSITE BELOW
*The Tenth Baron Cobham and his Family*, painted by an unknown artist. The pet parrot forms an exotic addition to this scene of Tudor domesticity.

from their boots, are accustomed to spread fresh rushes on the floors of all houses, on which they clean the soles of their shoes when they come in. This system is widely practised not only by Londoners but also by all the rest of the island's inhabitants, who, it seems, suffer from similar trouble from mud.

In some households woven rush mats which could be taken up all in one piece, cleaned, aired and put down again, began to replace the loose rushes. (The great Renaissance scholar Erasmus held dirty rushes to be one origin of the plague.) Some people favoured bare boards, well polished and with a rug or two, but carpets, home-made and imported, began to find favour towards the end of the sixteenth century.

Also coming into fashion was an apartment known as the long gallery which was built above stairs and often occupied the whole length of the house. It was a place in which the household could take exercise in really foul weather, where children could skip and whip their tops, and exercise their skill with cup-and-ball. Family portraits, rare at the beginning of the period but becoming more common later on, decorated the walls of the long gallery.

More privacy was possible in a Tudor house, though bedrooms often led out of one another. (If the bedrooms of an imposing house sometimes appear to be ill-proportioned, and slightly too small for the heavy four-poster with its canopy and curtains, it may be because in post-Tudor times interconnecting bedrooms fell from favour and each room had to sacrifice some space so that a passage could be made.) Servants were no longer expected to sleep on the floor of the hall; they were accommodated in the attics. Very gradually there was a move away from the use of the hall as a communal dining place except for times when many guests were to be entertained. The dining-room as we know it probably began with an apartment known as the Winter Parlour – a smaller, warmer place for family meals.

Windows were a feature of the new Tudor houses. They were often built so that they projected and let in light from three sides; the embrasure on the inside was sometimes too draughty to allow a candle to burn steadily within it. Hardwick Hall, 'more glass than wall', is the most famous example of this development. To some degree the loss of heat through the big windows was compensated by the insulating

OPPOSITE ABOVE Fire was a constant hazard, particularly in the overcrowded towns and cities, until brick and stone replaced wood as a building material. *The Fire of London, 1666,* by an artist of the Dutch school.

OPPOSITE BELOW In the seventeenth and eighteenth centuries coffee houses were a hotbed of political gossip and scandal, to which the drinking of this new and fashionable beverage formed a pleasant accompaniment. This painting is dated 1668.

RIGHT In many large houses, the hall was still the focal point. The Great Hall at Cotehele House, Cornwall, is furnished with benches and a trestle table bearing pewter plates. A large carved cupboard can be seen at the far end of the hall. The position of the table – close to the fire – would have been very necessary in such a large and draughty place.

OPPOSITE Henry VIII on his deathbed, with the young Edward VI. The philosophy behind this picture is that of the mortality of man – even of kings – and the permanence of God. The painting is particularly interesting for the visual details of bedding and night attire in Tudor times.

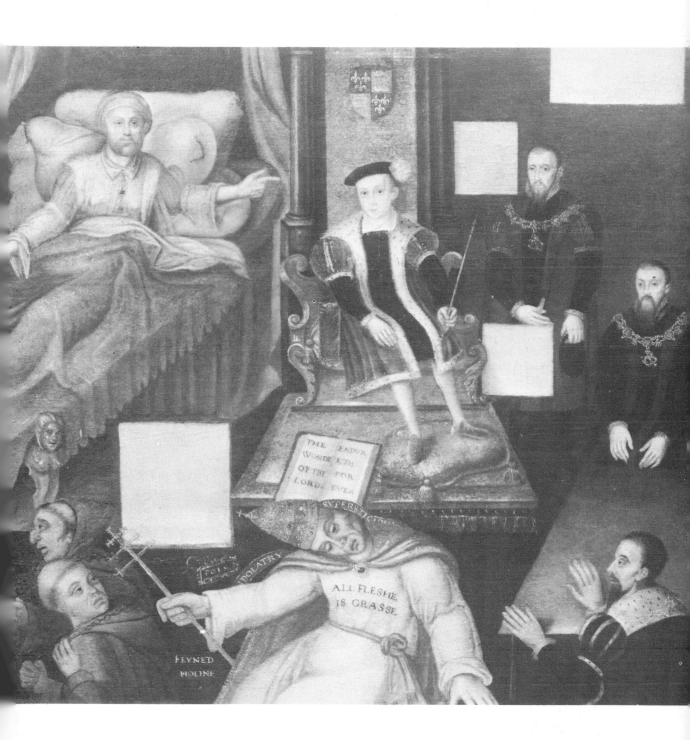

The more decorative aspect of Tudor beds is evident in this picture of the Green Velvet Bedroom at Hardwick Hall – named after the sumptuous hangings on the bed. The tapestries on the walls were imported from Flanders, long famous for its weaving, and, like the bed hangings, would also have served a practical purpose as draught excluders.

effect of panelling, some of which imitated, in wood, the cloth hangings which had decorated the cold stone walls of castles, and was therefore known as linenfold panelling. In great houses even the panelling was coloured and gilded, as were the elaborately moulded plaster ceilings.

The material used for building the house largely depended upon what was easily available in the district. The art of brickmaking had been rediscovered – Tudor bricks were smaller than modern ones – but where stone was plentiful, it was used. In well-wooded areas houses of some magnificence were still constructed of timber and plaster, the plaster often worked into decorative patterns by the process known as pargetting. Whatever the main fabric of the house, the chimneys were of brick, and seldom plain; the groups of ornamental chimneys are another distinctive Tudor feature.

The furniture of this period was chiefly of oak, heavy and solid, richly carved. Lidded chests were still in general use for storing clothes and linen, but the chest of drawers was making its first tentative appearance. It began as a drawer at the bottom of the clothes chest, and the advantage of having a separate compartment for flimsy, easily crushed articles was soon apparent. The well designed house had other storage space for clothes set in the thickness of the wall beside the chimney breast. Nowadays we would call them cupboards in England, but they were called closets then and the word went across the Atlantic and retained its meaning there. In England, and indeed over Western Europe the word 'closet' eventually had different associations, but not, unfortunately, for a couple of centuries.

The grandest house, the palace of Tudor times, was still a stranger to sanitation. The old garde-robe had gone; outside necessary houses still existed, and indoors one could find chamber pots and stool rooms furnished with stools or chairs with holes in their seats, and a bucket strategically placed under the hole. Some of these places of easement were designed to accommodate more than one person at once – the age was not coy about natural functions; nor, however, was it progressive, though it was given a positive lead by Sir John Harington, a godson of Queen Elizabeth. He made himself a water-flushed lavatory in his own home and a copy of it was installed for the Queen's use in Richmond Palace. Obviously she did not care for it; had she done so everybody would have wanted one. (She was such a trendsetter that she had made even red hair, formerly shunned because of its associations with prostitutes, all the rage.) For some reason Elizabeth, fastidious as she was, did not take to the contrivance which her godson called Ajax, and the water closet was shelved for a long time. The pot and bucket system went on. Most of the contents, in a well-ordered establishment, went into a cesspit, a hole dug in the earth. When it was full it was earthed or boarded in and a new one dug. In the middle of the nineteenth century when some reconstruction work was being done at Windsor Castle, fifty-three covered-in cesspits were discovered. Many great, though less well-known, establishments stood over or close to hidden sewers. Andrew Boorde's *Dyetary* published *c.* 1540 gives some useful advice on sanitation, but it is rather horrifying to think that it was necessary.

Furthermore, beware of pissing in draughts; and permit no common

Those with money could obviously afford to be open to new influences in building, and England's great houses show how these developments spread.

OPPOSITE Ightham Mote, Kent, begun in the mid-fourteenth century and extended in Tudor times, is clearly a house, not a castle, and yet still retains a defensive moat. Kent is famous for its many remaining half-timbered houses and barns – the Weald provided abundant supplies of wood for building.

ABOVE 'Hardwick Hall, more glass than wall' – Bess of Hardwick's splendid Derbyshire mansion, begun in 1590.

LEFT The Tudor brick and barley sugar chimneys of Compton Wynyates, Warwickshire. This house, the earliest parts of which date from the late fifteenth century, replaced an earlier house on the same site. The formal topiary is of great interest.

pissing place to be about the house or mansion; and let the common house of easement be over some water, or else elongated from the house. And beware of emptying pisspots and pissing in chimneys, so that all evil and contagious airs may be expelled, and clean air kept unputrified.

The mere carrying of pots and stool pails tainted the air; kitchens, however well screened, contributed unappetizing as well as appetizing odours, and some of the most decorative fireplaces, served by the most ornamental chimneys, belched smoke at times. By the end of a winter of close living, any house needed cleaning and airing. For the rich it was simple. Most of them owned two or three houses and could move from one to another, abandoning one house to be thoroughly cleaned and going to another, made ready, sweet and clean. Henry VIII and Elizabeth made what were known as progresses which brought them into the sight of thousands of adoring subjects, even if they sometimes bankrupted their hosts. But the vast majority of people had only one home and that was as much in need of thorough cleaning as a palace. The single house had to be subjected to the frenzied activity whose name still survives – spring cleaning. Windows were opened, every washable surface washed, feather beds and pillows exposed to the sun – supposed to be death to vermin – and sometimes even split open and plucked over.

Now that it was no longer necessary for a large house to be fortified, and thus restricted to small defensible grounds, gardens became possible and popular. The Tudor people brought to this new art all the energy and the lively curiosity that was typical of the period. English ships and English traders were ranging the world and plants were among the discoveries they brought home. A good many exotic ones must have been tried in Tudor gardens; some failed, but some, like the geranium, flourished. Some plants now common in the English garden – the wistaria is one – had to wait awhile, for they grew in China, still unknown territory.

The grand house had a grand garden, laid out on formal lines, with paths and flowerbeds bordered by low hedges of yew, rosemary or lavender. Some yews were allowed to grow tall and then clipped into the shape of birds and beasts to form a topiary. Yew, being a thick-growing plant, was also used for making yew walks, sheltered from the wind, and for mazes. If water were easily available the garden would have fountains. All these things reflected the Italian influence, for more people went to Italy in this period than ever before. (Shakespeare plainly disapproved and said, 'The Englishman Italianate is the Devil incarnate.') The gardens that ran down to the banks of the Thames behind the palatial houses in the Strand in London, and were served by their own private stairs to the water, were of this type; and Hampton Court is a good example of a formal, geometric garden.

The ordinary garden was a far more haphazard combination of the ornamental with the useful. The form can still be seen in really old country gardens where onions and lilies grow side by side in comfortable companionship. Most Tudor gardens were walled – the term 'close' was often applied to them – and on a south-facing wall apricots, peaches, plums and pears could be ripened to perfection in a good summer, but the well-to-do were starting to grow grapes, apricots, peaches and even oranges under glass. Quinces and medlars, both hardy, were common then.

Somewhere in the vicinity of a really grand house there would be a covered court in which tennis could be played – the court used by Henry VIII can still be seen at Hampton Court. It was then a different game from the one we know: the court could be of a size governed by the space available, and players could use their hands or a gut-strung racket according to choice. Played with solid balls, it must have been a hazardous game, but ladies and children are reputed to have enjoyed it.

Behind the gracious facade of the Tudor houses a more domesticated style of family life was developing, partly due to the peace and stability of the age, and partly to the civilizing influence of Renaissance ideas and to the growing popularity of domestic amusements such as reading, conversation, gardening and musicmaking. Erasmus has left a pleasant picture of the family of Sir Thomas More in the reign of Henry VIII. He wrote to a friend: 'More hath builte near London upon the Thames side, a commodius house, neither meane nor subject to envie, yet magnificent enough; there he converseth affably with his family, his wife, his son and daughter-in-lawe, his three daughters and their husbands, with eleven grandchildren.'

FAMILIA THOMÆ M

Thomas Morus Aᵒ. 50. Alicia Thomæ Mori uxor Aᵒ. 57. Iohannes Morus pater Aᵒ. 76. Iohannes Morus Th
Elisabeta Danea Thomæ Mori filia Aᵒ. 21. Cæcilia Heroina Thomæ Mori filia Aᵒ. 20. Margareta Giga Cl

This pen and ink drawing of the family of Sir Thomas More, by Holbein, formed the basis of a subsequent painting. The Latin inscription at the bottom names the various members of his family present.

ANGL : CANCELL :

A°.19. Anna Grisacria Iohannis Mori Sponsa A°.15. Margareta Ropera Thomæ Mori filia A°.22.
r Mori filiabus Condiscipula et cognata A°.22. Henricus Patensonus Thomæ Mori morio A°.40.

It was common for a house to contain more than the immediate family: it was a haven for any relation who through widowhood, or failure to marry, or loss of parents, was in need of a home.

Children were still strictly brought up but the relationship with their parents seems to have become more affectionate. Even Elizabeth's stern secretary, William Cecil, could write a charming poem to his daughter Ann accompanying the gift of a spinning wheel.

> But one thing first I wish and pray,
> Lest thirst of thrift might soon you tire
> Only to spin one pound a day
> And play the rest as time require.

His affection was not strong enough to turn him from the advantages of marrying her to a young wastrel, the Earl of Oxford, but he did welcome Ann and her children back to his roof when the marriage broke up. When Cecil was an old man it was said of him: 'If he could get his table set round with young children he was then in his kingdom. He was happy in most worldly things, but most happy in his children and children's children.'

Boys were still sent away from home, but more often to school and university to be educated in the arts and sciences than to a noble household to learn the art of war, as had been the medieval custom. The gentry were not ashamed to apprentice their younger sons to trade and this helped to avert the deep division between the classes which occurred on the Continent, where an idle nobility scorned to dabble in business. In later centuries a certain snobbishness did set in against trade but Tudor England had the advantage of 'making gentlemen so easily', as a contemporary commented.

Books became more plentiful in Tudor households, thanks to the industry of William Caxton whose presses poured out a hundred books before the end of the fifteenth century. Popular titles were Aesop's *Fables*, Malory's *Morte d'Arthur* and the works of Chaucer. Printing also encouraged musicmaking in the home as songs and madrigals became more cheaply and easily available. Between 1588 and 1630 over eighty collections of songs by composers such as Morley, Dowland and Campion were printed. Singing became so fashionable that it was

an essential accomplishment for any gentleman. In 1597 Thomas Morley describes an embarrassing incident in his *Plaine and Easie Introduction to Practicale Musicke*:

Supper being ended, and musicke bookes (according to the custom) being brought to table, the mistresse of the house presented me with a part, earnestly requesting me to sing; but when, after many excuses, I protested unfainedly that I could not, every one began to wonder! Yes, some whispered to others, demanding how I was brought up; so that upon shame of mine ignorance, I goe now to seek out mine old friend Master Gnorimus to make myself his scholler.

Dancing and music were very popular in Tudor times. Here Queen Elizabeth, dances with one of her courtiers. The extravagant and exaggerated fashions of the late sixteenth century are much in evidence.

To make Limon Marmalott.

Take Limons halve them and Squeeze out the juice and boyle them very tender
as you doe Orange Pill to Peree but you must not past them till they be boyled
then cutt them in thin small peices then take doth Apples pare them e cutt them
into over the bignes of Limons then weigh the Limons e to ¼ lb of Limon take
¼ lb of Apple soe cutt 1 lb of double refind Sugar beaten very fine e putt to a full pint
of water sett it upon the fire e lett it boyle then putt in the Limon e Apple e keep
it boyling as fast as you can till it look cleare then putt in six Spoonfulls of the
Juice of Limon e boyle it a little while after when it is a little coole glass it up
Shift the water in boyling the peel and lett not the Marmalade be boyling hott
when you putt the raw juice in lett it boyle but a very little or only Scald after it
is in becaule the Limon is apt to look with white Specks.

Food was a great pleasure to the people of Tudor England, as foreigners were quick to note. The Italian Andreas Franciscus described in 1497 how the common people 'delight in banquets and variety of meat and food, and they excel everyone in preparing them with an excessive abundance. They eat very frequently, at times more than is suitable, and are particularly fond of young swans, rabbits, deer and seabirds.' By common people he presumably meant citizens and yeomen, for there would have been no 'excessive abundance' in the homes of the labourers. Bread, bacon, cheese and beer or cider would have been the staple diet in a poor home, with meat once or twice a week if they were lucky.

Fifty years later the pleasures of the stomach had not grown less popular, according to a scornful Spaniard who accompanied Philip of Spain to the court of Queen Mary in 1554:

> There are no distractions here except eating and drinking, the only variety they understand. . . . There is plenty of beer here and they drink more than would fill the Valladolid river. In summer the ladies and some gentlemen put sugar in their wine, with the result that there are great goings on in the palace.

A new vegetable was introduced to English diet in the reign of Elizabeth – the potato, brought back from America by Sir Walter Raleigh. He had an estate in Ireland and the potato was first cultivated on a large scale there. On the whole the climate and the soil suited it, and 'Ireland's lazy root' became so much the staple diet that the failure of one year's crop could bring famine to the country. In England it made slower progress, was grown as a garden vegetable rather than as a field crop and was far more popular, to begin with, in the north than in the south. It is difficult now to imagine life without it.

Raleigh was also responsible for introducing into England the 'noxious weed' tobacco which he had observed giving pleasure to the natives of the New World. The habit caught on, but strictly for men only – who could imagine a woman with a clay pipe in her mouth? Men found the process soothing and companionable. It was not until the next reign that we find the first fulminations against smoking, written by King James himself: 'Herein is not only a great vanity, but a great

OPPOSITE ABOVE Sixteenth-century cutlery. In spite of the delicate engraving and inlay work on the handles, the knives are clearly very basic and functional in design, and the fork – long considered an effeminate foreign invention – is still notable by its absence.

OPPOSITE BELOW A recipe for 'Limon Marmalott', or lemon marmalade as we would call it today.

OPPOSITE
Elizabethan costume may have had its ridiculous and impractical aspects, but it could also be extremely beautiful. This painting by Hieronimo Custodis, entitled *Elizabeth Brydges, Lady Kennedy*, shows a wealth of exquisite detail in the lace ruff, the lavish embroidery of the dress, and the more delicate work on the cuffs.

contempt of God's good gifts, that the sweetness of man's breath . . . should be wilfully corrupted by this stinking smoke.' He imposed heavy duties on the import of tobacco for social as well as economic reasons.

In fashion ostentation was the hallmark of the Tudor period. Never before and never again was such sheer extravagance seen in the way of clothes; the richest material was lavishly embroidered and studded with precious stones. Two dresses, one for each of his daughters, cost one doting father £1,500. (Few people have attempted an exact conversion scale, but this was at a time when a country mansion could be built for £5,000, and a man with an income of £40 a year was looked upon as a substantial citizen.) Critics of the day complained that women walked about with the worth of two manors around their necks. Unmarried women had a good deal of space upon which to display their jewels, for the custom of the day allowed virgins to expose their breasts; married women were expected to be rather more modest. Elizabeth Tudor, most admirable of women in many ways, was what one might call a professional virgin and took such advantage of this fashion that one shocked visitor reported that when she leaned forward he could practically see her navel.

Over a period of 118 years fashions altered, of course, but the general trend was towards a rigidity, an artificiality hitherto unknown. The medieval lady had nipped in her waist; by Elizabeth I's time women of fashion were nipping in their whole torsos and wearing bodices of which the narrow lowest point was almost on the pelvis. Below, from hip to heel, skirts spread wide, held out by stiffly starched petticoats, or a wire cage called a farthingale. It is fortunate that the appearance of these gorgeous if ridiculous clothes coincided with the development of portrait painting, which has left numerous dazzling records of Tudor fashions.

Men's clothes – for those who wished to be considered part of the fashionable world – were equally extravagant, with enormous sleeves and breeches stuffed with wool or bran, and that slightly obscene appendage the codpiece, jewelled and embroidered to draw attention to the wearer's virility. A man anxious to cut a dash at court would pawn an estate in order to buy an eye-taking jewel for his cap. A

ÆTATIS SVÆ . 14 ...
ANNO DÑi . 1589 ...

Elizabeth Bruges daughter
to the Lord Giles Chandos

Venetian diplomat, Pasqualigo, has left a vivid impression of Henry VIII and his court in 1515 when the King was in the prime of young manhood and not the gross pasty-faced figure he became later on.

He wore a cap of crimson velvet, in the French fashion, and the brim was looped up all around with lacets, which had gold enamelled tags. His doublet was in the French fashion, striped alternately with white and crimson satin, and his hose were scarlet and all slashed from the knee upwards. . . . His mantel was of purple velvet, lined with white satin, the sleeves being open, and with a train verily more than four Venetian yards in length. This mantle was girt in front like a gown, with a thick gold cord from which hung glands entirely of gold; over this mantle was a very handsome gold collar, with a pendant of St George, entirely of diamonds. . . . To the right of his majesty were eight noblemen dressed like himself . . . and moreover a crowd of nobility, all arrayed in cloth of gold and silk.

Two illustrations from books on hunting. In an age when books were still owned only by the privileged few, hunting was obviously a subject of major interest.

OPPOSITE From *The booke of Hunting*, an illustration entitled 'Of the place where and howe an assembly should be made, in the presence of a Prince, or some honorable person' depicts a rather lavish picnic. It is doubtful whether the two greedy figures in the foreground are observing the correct etiquette required for the occasion!

LEFT Illustration from the title page of *The Noble Art of Venerie or Hunting*.

The most extraordinary fashion of all was the ruff. It began with a standing collar, starched and edged with lace, and ended as a stiffly pleated wheel, in extreme cases fifteen inches in radius. This made eating difficult and there is mention of specially long-handled spoons. Men and married women could have their necks entirely encircled, but the maiden state must be proclaimed by keeping the throat and bosom exposed and wearing the ruff only as far forward as the shoulders. This upset its balance, and it had to be supported by struts of metal or whalebone. The ruffs were washed, dipped into a solution of flour and water and then pleated by the application of heated tongs. At the height of the fashion hundreds of women on the outskirts of London earned their bread by caring for ruffs, a process which demanded plenty of water, clean air and space for bleaching and drying. Piccadilly was one of these areas and is said to have taken its name from the business, though strictly speaking the term 'picadil' applied rather to a shoulder ornament than to the ruff.

The wealth which paid for the fine new houses, extravagant clothes and gargantuan meals came mainly from a more economic use of agricultural land, enabling the country to produce a surplus above the needs of subsistence, which fed the towns and was traded abroad. This was achieved by the enclosure of waste land, demesne land, common land or open-field strips into large arable fields or pasture for sheep. As a result many peasants (nearly all of them were now freemen) were evicted from their smallholdings, or lost their rights to the common land, and labourers were put out of work in the areas where enclosure for pasture took place for sheep farming required a smaller work force. The numbers concerned were small compared with those who were to suffer in the eighteenth-century enclosures, but to concerned observers it seemed as if a whole way of life was being broken up. Sir Thomas More protested that 'Sheep eateth men' and in his *Utopia* published in 1516 he described the fate of the peasant farmers:

The husbandmen be thrust oute of their owne, or els either by coveyne and fraude, or by violent oppression they be put besydes it, or by wronges and injuries thei be so weried that they be compelled to sell all: by one means therfore or by other, either by hooke or crooke they must needes depart awaye, poore, selye, wretched soules.

This detail from a late sixteenth-century tapestry table carpet shows various aspects of hunting, and gives an idea of the kinds of meat eaten in those days. The man on the left is about to take a pot-shot at either a swan or a heron.

Within the image: S. PAULES CHURCH, Bow Church, THAMESIS

A panoramic view of London and the Thames shows its skyline dominated by church spires and old St Paul's Cathedral. On the right is Old London Bridge with its huddle of medieval dwellings built on the bridge itself.

The situation was not improved by the dissolution of the monasteries in the reign of Henry VIII when nearly one-fifteenth of the countryside passed into the hands of new owners, concerned chiefly to enrich themselves and not bound by the medieval concept of responsibility for their tenants. The higher standard of living enjoyed by the majority of the population in Elizabeth's reign was therefore only achieved at the expense of many of the poorest class who were turned off the land. Some went to swell the towns, others to swell the new class of beggars and vagabonds. By the second half of the century the problem of poverty was so great that Parliament was forced to recognize it in the Poor Law which made parishes responsible for providing employment or subsistence for the unemployed.

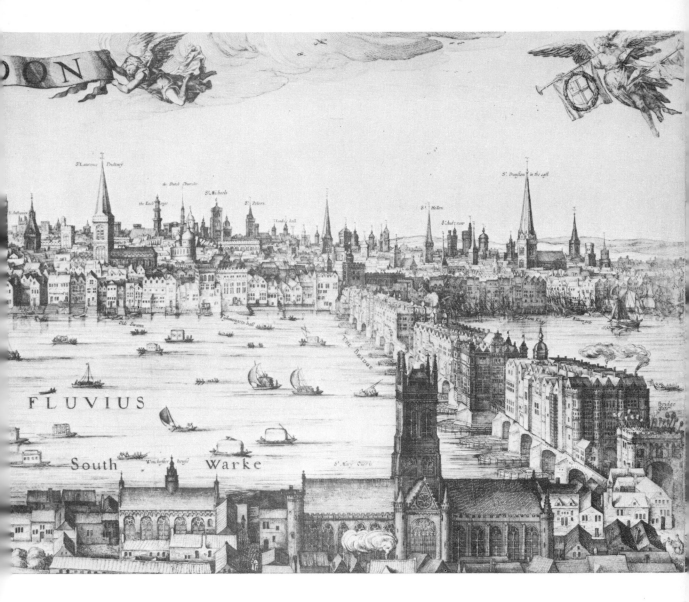

The increase in the standard of living of all but the lowest classes drew the attention of contemporary writers. Feather beds, for example, were becoming common, whereas in the past, as William Harrison wrote in 1577: 'Our fathers yea and we ourselves have lain full oft upon straw pallets, covered only with a sheet, under coverlets made of dagswain or hop harlots (I use their own terms) and a good round log under their head instead of a bolster.' Other changes noted were the numbers of fireplaces erected and the replacement of wooden plates by pewter. The will of a yeoman, Thomas Quenell, in 1571, gives some indication of the considerable household goods possessed by this class. Here is a selection of the effects that Quenell wished to leave to his wife:

*The Family of the Third Earl of Windsor*, painted in 1568 by an unknown artist. The elderly woman on the right has made no attempt to keep pace with fashion, while the Countess (centre) certainly has. It was still an age of early marriage for girls – the Countess's age is given as twenty-five, and that of the eldest of her four sons as eight.

. . . my three beste beddes with boulsters pyllowes and pyllowe coate belonging to them, my best bedstedle (except one) all my sheate (excepte three payer of canvas sheate, all my beste blanckete (except one payer), my three best coverlette and one Qwylte, all my pewter vessyll, (except fyve pewter platters twoe pewter disshes and one basone which were my fathers), my beste and my leaste twoe candlestyck, my beste brasse potts, my beste and my leaste twoe kettles, and my kettle whiche was bound with yron by Hewghe the Smythe, my posnet of belle brasse, my leaste Skyllet of brasse and the occupacon of my Cawdron as often as she shall have nede . . . twoe of my beste table clothes, twoe of my beste towels, half of all my table napkyns, one dozen of my beste spons, my three best soup cuppes, the beste cheste . . . and all the resedue of my cofers. . . .

William Harrison thought all this luxury had weakened the fibres of the English people and made them 'altogether of straw'. 'Now we have many chimneys,' he wrote, 'and yet our tenderlings complain of rheums, catarrhs and poses.' However, from a modern viewpoint the life of the yeoman farmer still appears a hard one – manual work from dawn to dusk and all effort brought to nothing by a spell of bad weather. And look what was expected of the yeoman's wife in Anthony Fitzherbert's *Boke of Husbandry*, 1523:

And when though art up and ready, then first sweep thy house, dress up thy dishboard, and set all things in good order within thy house: milk thy kye, suckle thy calves, syc up thy milk, take up thy children and array them, and provide for thy husband's breakfast, dinner, supper and for thy children and servants, and take thy part with them. And to ordain corn and malt to the mill, to bake and brew withal when need is. . . . Thou must make butter and cheese when thou mayest, serve thy swine both morning and evening, and give thy poultry meat in the morning. . . . And in the beginning of March, or a little before, it time for a wife to make her garden, and to get as many good seeds and herbs as she can, and specially such as be good for the pot, and to eat.

After further advice on the cultivation of flax and hemp, spinning and weaving, the author gives a somewhat unnecessary warning: 'Let thy distaff be always ready for a pastime, that thou be not idle.' One feels the people of Tudor England really earned their feather beds.

Elizabeth, last of the Tudors, fought off death as resolutely as she had tried to fight off old age. But she was only mortal and in the seventieth year of her life, the forty-fifth of her reign, she died, leaving a legend. She was devious and wilful and perverse; with more than a thousand costly dresses in her wardrobe she had sent her seamen to face the Spanish Armada short of ammunition and even of food. But to the ordinary person that was irrelevant, to them she had brought peace and prosperity; she had stabilized the currency and halted rising prices, and steered a middle course in the troubled question of religion. It was not only her courtiers and officials who felt that things would never be the same again after her death; the man in the street and the man in the field felt that too. And they were right. Only the powerful personality and charm of Elizabeth had kept parliaments reasonably acquiescent until the end of the sixteenth century. Her successor James I had too little charm and too much sense of his divine right to rule; a struggle for power was inevitable.

# 4 Puritans and Periwigs

he Civil War of 1642–7 was to affect the life of the people in a far more direct manner than had the recurrent struggles between king and lords in the Middle Ages. For the Civil War was not only a battle for power but a clash of ideologies, and the ideology of the victors extended to the sort of clothes people should wear. Politically the seeds of conflict were soon apparent in the disagreements between James I and his parliaments; domestically life went on in much the same way as it had under Elizabeth, right up to the Civil War.

One change occurred in building styles as a direct result of the new reign. James I had a particular fear of fire, and saw that timber-framed houses with their upper storey projecting below the lower, so that from their bedroom windows women could touch hands, were a definite fire hazard. James forbade such building. He was not always obeyed, but as a rough rule of thumb any building with a projecting upper floor may be dated as earlier than 1605. There were other changes in building styles, too; a little less individuality and exuberance, a more classical style, fostered by the emergence of a new profession, that of architect – the man who designed but did not build houses. A visit to Italy was an essential experience for any aspiring architect. Such a man might design and oversee personally the building of only a few houses, but the new ideas spread through imitation and the handing about of sketches and descriptions. For the first time since Saxon days the lofty great hall was no longer the centre of the house. Several smaller rooms only one storey high took its place and these became decorated with panelling rather than tapestry. Ornamental plaster-work decorated the ceilings. The courtyard round which earlier houses had been built was moved behind the new buildings.

During the early years of James I's reign, fashions in clothes changed little, and slowly. Those changes that were made were in the direction of moderation, both the ruff and the width of the farthingale becoming smaller. Towards the end of the reign the ruff had fallen into a lace collar – the 'fallen ruff', and the farthingale had disappeared, leaving the skirt to be supported by petticoats only. The outer petticoat was of material too fine in itself, or too richly embroidered, to be entirely

OPPOSITE This detail of Van Dyck's painting *The Five Children of Charles I* shows, despite the satins and lace, a certain delightful informality.

Seventeenth-century interiors.

ABOVE Life-size dummy-board figures were often found in Stuart drawing-rooms.

RIGHT The Long Gallery at Blickling Hall, Norfolk, with its superb Jacobean plaster ceiling.

OPPOSITE The Marble Dining-Room at Ham House, Richmond, contains sturdy Stuart furniture made in English woods. Furniture styles were to change dramatically in the next century with the introduction of exotic woods such as mahogany, and under foreign – notably French – influence.

hidden, so the skirt of the gown was slashed and shaped to display the undergarment. The rigidity and extent of the corset were greatly reduced, resulting in a more natural, easy look. The elaborate, high-dressed coiffure gave way to falling ringlets, for men as well as women. It was no longer necessary to wear every jewel one owned at the same time; bows and knots of ribbon were considered sufficient decoration.

However the Civil War was won not by the ringleted supporters of Charles I but by Cromwell's 'plain, russet-coated captains', whose cropped hair had given them the name of Roundheads. Only the most

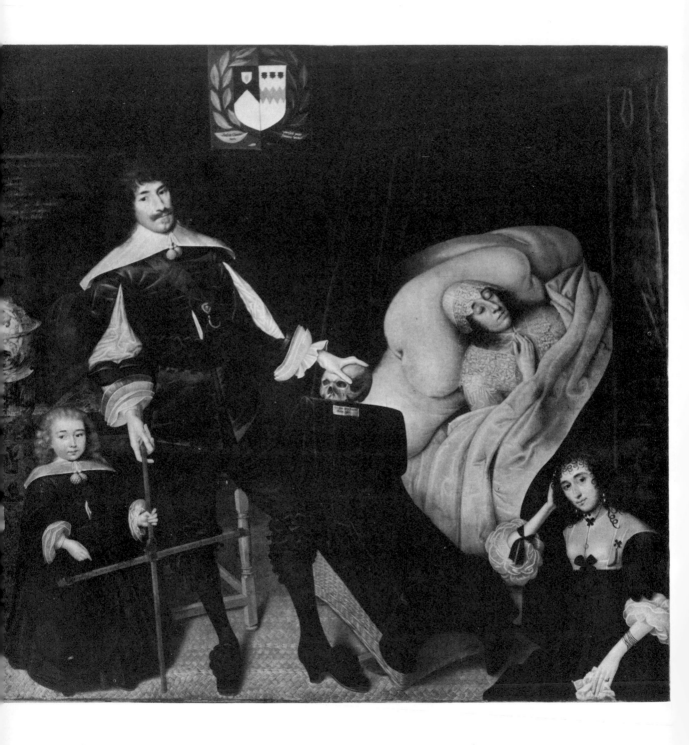

foolhardy of royalists dared flaunt cavalier costume in the years of Puritan supremacy between the execution of Charles I in 1649 and the restoration of his son in 1660. Fashion came to a standstill and all clothes followed the same utilitarian style. Woollen stuff replaced silk and velvet, collars and cuffs were of linen, not lace, jewellery was put away. Men's hair was cropped in roundhead style, women smoothed their hair back into demure little knobs. Black, grey and buff were the acceptable colours and even women who did not necessarily do housework were expected to wear a white apron, like a farm wife's.

Drabness permeated all aspects of life. Theatres and alehouses were closed, certain games and sports were forbidden and the celebration of Christmas was outlawed as 'Papist'. People were not even allowed to go to church on Christmas Day, as John Evelyn noted in his diary in 1652: 'There being no churches to attend, nor any public assembley, I was obliged to pass the devotions of this blessed day with my family at home.' Cromwell's soldiers roamed the streets of London to make sure that no festivities were held.

Perhaps to ordinary people the saddest loss was the disappearance of Sunday as a merry holiday. Before the Puritans came to power sports and dancing had taken place after the morning service, as the presbyterian Richard Baxter remembered: 'In the village where I lived the Reader read the Common Prayer briefly and the rest of the day was spent in dancing under the maypole. . . .' The Puritans forbade all recreation on Sundays and offered instead enormously long sermons; one is said to have lasted four hours. The gaiety of an English Sunday was one thing that never recovered from the Puritan onslaught. In the reign of the last Stuart, Queen Anne, a German visitor was depressed by the Sabbath quiet:

In the afternoon to St James's Park, to see the crowds. No other diversion is allowed on Sunday, which is nowhere more strictly kept; not only is all play forbidden, and public-houses closed, but few even of the boats and hackney coaches may ply. Our hostess would not even allow the strangers to play the viol di Gamba or the flute lest she be punished.

It is strange to think that a youth of eighteen or so at the time of the Restoration would never have been to a play, never have seen churches

OPPOSITE *Sir Thomas Aston at the Deathbed of His Wife*, painted by John Souch in 1635–6. The black-draped cradle, on which Sir Thomas is resting a 'memento mori' skull, suggests that she may have died in childbirth. The painting gives an excellent idea of the costume and hairstyles of pre-Cromwellian England. Note the woven rush matting on the floor.

ABOVE Engraving of the very large family of 'Sir Thomas Remmington of Lund in the East Riding of the County of York'.

OPPOSITE A pair of seventeenth-century dolls – Lord and Lady Clapham.

enriched with altar cloths or priests in their vestments, and would scarcely remember houses decorated with holly and ivy for Christmas. No wonder that in 1660 Samuel Pepys noted in his diary 'All the world in a merry mood because of the King's coming.' All but the most earnest Puritans were tired of lives regulated by a stern religion and eager to welcome back the pleasure-loving Charles II, the Merry Monarch.

Beautiful clothes were the vogue again; still much in the style of the pre-Puritan period. (Had some been carefully laid away?) There were

fewer jewels; many had been sold to keep the Civil War going, and then to finance exiles. Cosmetics were allowed once more and again all women of fashion managed to look alike. One thing that was new was the wig, originally the product of necessity. Women could loosen their tightly knobbed hair and make curls at a moment's notice but men with cropped heads needed wigs before they could face Charles II, who wore his hair in the old Cavalier style. Wigs had existed before this time, but had been worn only by women like Elizabeth Tudor who resented what age had done to their natural hair; Mary Queen of Scots had worn one too. Now every man must have one and there was a great demand for hair, preferably from the head of a healthy live young woman, but at a pinch from a dead body. Samuel Pepys hesitated a long time before taking to wigs – could they have come from the heads of Plague victims? But at last the bother of keeping his hair clean, and the news that the King was to have one, brought him to the point:

Home, and by and by comes Chapman, the peri-wigg maker, and upon my liking it without more ado I went up, and there he cut off my haire, which went a little to my heart at present to part with it; but, it being over, and my periwigg on, I paid him £3 for it; and away went he, with my own haire, to make up another of; and I, by and by, went abroad, after I had caused all my maids to look upon it; and they conclude it do become me; though Jane was mightily troubled for my parting of my owne haire, and so was Besse.

The wig-stand, a faceless skull of wood at the top of a stick high enough to allow the curls to flow, became part of the bedroom furniture and some can be still seen in old churches where the priest in charge might divest himself on hot oppressive days if he felt so inclined.

The reaction against the Puritan way of life led to another development, the Pleasure Garden, a place where people could meet and stroll, take refreshment and be entertained. Of these Vauxhall was the most famous, but there were a number of others. At first these were pleasant, well-conducted places which even the most respectable women were not ashamed to frequent, properly escorted. There was a new delicacy to be tasted, ice cream, and splendid firework displays. But inevitably such gardens attracted prostitutes seeking custom and men in search of bought pleasure; and gradually the places became disreputable. Vauxhall was closed, appropriately, in Victorian days.

Another meeting place was the coffee house. The first had been set up by an enterprising Turk in 1652 to introduce the new beverage. It was so successful that similar places sprang up all over London and many provincial towns could boast at least one. They became more than places of refreshment; they were more like clubs, where men could meet and talk business and discuss the latest news. Chocolate – the produce of the West Indian cocoa tree – was first tried as a novelty in an established coffee house, and tea was introduced to the public in the same way. Gradually all three became part of every well-to-do household's expenditure. Hot chocolate must be served in a special covered cup – a few beautiful examples survive – and tea-drinking took on a ceremonial ritual, demanding not only its own china but its own tray, its own table, and its own securely locked container called a caddy, which derived its name from *kati*, a Malayan measure of weight.

All tea at this time came from China and was very expensive indeed, for only the Dutch East India Company had reached China. It is said that some of the lovely lacquered cabinets which are now so greatly treasured came into this country simply as tea-containers, the contents being so valuable that decorative packaging could be afforded. It was suitable that with the tea should come the delicate bowls from which tea was drunk in its native place. They had no handles then – one was invited to take a dish of tea. Such valuable things could not be trusted to the ham-fisted servant to wash up, and it was customary for a bowl of hot water and a cloth to be brought to the mistress of the house so that she could do the job herself.

Because tea was so costly it became a kind of status symbol. Vestigial echoes of it remain to this day, though few of the kind women who will offer even a stranger a 'cuppa' are conscious of being privileged, and willing to share their privilege. The price of tea fell rapidly when the British East India Company reached China and when tea-planting began in India itself and in Ceylon; but the price – £1 a pound, including heavy import duty – still put it out of reach of the ordinary person. Most tea-leaves were brewed three times: first for the mistress of the house, her family and guests; then for the servants; then the leaves were carefully saved and partially dried and passed on to relatives or friends of the servants.

Sugar could be used to improve the flavour of tea, coffee and chocolate because it became much cheaper and more plentiful during the seventeenth century. This enabled housewives to preserve fruit in the form of jam with an inch-thick layer of mutton fat to keep the jars airtight. Some choice fruits, and rose petals and violets, could be crystallized and used as decorations for cakes and puddings. A by-product of sugar was rum, perhaps the first spiritous liquor to take hold in England. Sailors had found it a guard against conditions of extreme cold and it first became popular as a medicine, well whisked with butter.

A detailed picture of the domestic life of a middle-class family in Restoration England is preserved in the fascinating diaries of Samuel Pepys. He was the son of a tailor but through the patronage of his father's more elevated cousin, the Earl of Sandwich, and through his own abilities, he became in 1660 'clerk of the King's ships' and clerk of

This woodcut of rural life, dated c. 1650, shows a woman spinning and two men hunting a stag.

the privy seal, with a salary of £350 per annum supplemented by fees and bribes. He began his diary in 1660 when he was twenty-six and continued it for nine years, until his sight began to fail. He wrote for himself and not for posterity and the diary is particularly entertaining because it contains all the human follies, vices and self-doubts which more sophisticated diarists have omitted. In the early years of the diary Pepys is struggling to improve his financial position and takes a great pleasure in his growing wealth, whether expressed in his clothes, his house or his plate:

Up, and put things in order against dinner. I out and bought some things: among others, a dozen of silver salts: and at noon comes my company. . . . They eyed mightily my great cupboard of plate – I this day putting my two flaggons upon my table; and indeed it is a fine sight, and better than ever I did hope to see of my own.

Clothes accounted for a large part of Pepys's expenditure. At a time when his household costs were only £7 a month, one pair of gloves for his wife cost £1: 'Called upon Doll, our pretty 'Change woman, for a pair of gloves trimmed with yellow ribbon to [match] the petticoat my wife bought yesterday, which cost me 20s, but she is so pretty that, God forgive me! I could not think it too much.' Pepys was often concerned at the amount he spent on clothes but considered it essential to his position: 'I find that I must go handsomely, whatever it costs me, and the charge will be made up in the fruits it brings.' But one suspects he was seeking to excuse the cost of his own vanity, for the diary is peppered with entries such as 'Out, to show my new suit'.

When they were alone the Pepyses dined quite simply off 'a good hog's harslet' or 'a good pie baked of a leg of mutton' but when guests came a great spread was offered:

My poor wife rose by five o'clock in the morning before day, and went to market and bought fowles and many other things for dinner, with which I was highly pleased, and the chine of beef was down also before six o'clock, and my owne jacke, of which I was doubtfulle, do carry it very well, things being put in order, and the cook come. By and by comes Dr Clerke and his lady, his sister, and a she-cosen, and Mr Pierce and his wife, which was all my guests. I had for them, after oysters, at first course, a hash of rabbits and lamb, and a rare chine of beef. Next, a great dish of roasted fowle, cost me

*To bake a Carp according to these Forms to be eaten hot.*

Take a carp, scale it, and scrape off the slime, bone it, and cut it into dice-work, the milt being parboild, cut it into the same form, then have some great oysters parboild and cut in the same form also ; put to it some grapes, gooseberries, or barberries, the bottoms of artichocks boild the yolks of hard eggs in quarters, boild sparagus cut an inch long, and some pistaches, season all the foresaid things together with pepper, nutmegs, and salt, fill the pyes, close them up, and bake them, being baked, liquor them with butter, white-wine, and some blood of the carp, boil them together, or beaten butter with juyce of oranges.

*To bake a Carp with Eels to be eaten cold.*

Take four large carps, scale them and wipe off the slime clean, bone them, and cut each side into two pieces of every carp, then have four large fresh water eels, fat ones,
boned

about 30s, and a tart, and then fruit and cheese. My dinner was noble, and enough. . . . I believe this day's feast will cost me near £5.

Because of the grandeur of this dinner a cook was specially employed. Normally Mrs Pepys managed with a varying number of living-in servants. When the diary begins there is only 'servant Jane', but as the Pepyses become more prosperous their staff increases. At the end of 1664 Samuel was able to record:

My family is my wife, in good health, and happy with her; her woman Mercer, a pretty, modest, quiet maid; her chambermaid Besse, her cook-maid Jane, the little girl Susan, and my boy, which I have had about half a year, Tom Edwards, which I took from the King's Chapel; and as pretty and loving quiet a family I have as any man in England.

In 1660 Pepys moved into a new house and spent a great deal of time

OPPOSITE A recipe for baking carp, from *The Accomplisht Cook* by Robert May, published in 1671. In the days before refrigeration, carp, a freshwater fish, would have been safer and more palatable than sea fish which had been transported from the coast.

LEFT This engraving of a seventeenth-century kitchen shows meat roasting on a spit, game hanging from the ceiling, a cook rolling out pastry, a pie dish in the shape of a peacock (right), and, in the foreground, a cat advancing inexorably on a plate of fish.

and money improving it: 'All afternoon among my workmen, and did give them drink, and very merry with them, it being my luck to meet with a sort of drolling workmen on all occasions.' The dining-room was finished 'with green serge hanging and gilt leather, which is very handsome', the parlour was panelled, and £5 was spent on pictures for decoration. Mrs Pepys had some trouble with the oven: 'Found my wife making of pies and tarts to try her oven with, but now knowing the nature of it, did heat it too hot, and so a little overbake her things, but knows how to do it better another time.'

The recreations of the Pepyses were typical of the time. They went frequently to the theatre and aired themselves in Hyde Park to mingle with the fashionable world; they watched executions, and took river jaunts to Greenwich and crossed London Bridge to pick cowslips in the meadows south of the river. Samuel Pepys also went frequently to coffee houses and nearly as frequently got drunk.

I took my flageolette and played upon the leads in the garden, where Sir W. Pen come out in his shirt into his leads, and there we staid talking and singing and drinking great draughts of claret, and eating botargo [a type of sausage] and bread and butter till twelve at night, it being moonshine; and so to bed, very near fuddled.

On another occasion he admits being so drunk that he went to bed 'without prayers, which I never did yet, since I come to the house, of a Sunday night: I being now so out of order that I durst not read prayers for fear of being perceived by the servants in what case I was.' At the end of 1660 he takes 'a solemn oath about abstaining from plays and wine' which goes the way of all New Year resolutions.

In his intellectual pursuits Pepys displays the vigour which was noticeable in this age and which led to the founding of the Royal Society. He learned several musical instruments and tried his hand at composing; he studied arithmetic and taught it to his wife; he bought two globes to study at home and spent a great deal of money on books. A quiet evening was passed in learning the speech 'To be or not to be' by heart. Indeed he seems to have led a full and merry life, though always aspiring to a more lavish life-style: 'Talked long in bed with my wife, about our frugal life for the time to come, proposing to her what I

The habits of Jacobean men probably did not always please their families.

LEFT An alehouse scene.

BELOW A Jacobean gentleman lights up a pipe of that newly discovered weed, tobacco, much to the consternation of his wife and children.

could and would do, if I were worth £2000, that is, be a knight and keep my coach, which pleased her.'

The Pepyses had no children, so for an account of this side of domestic life we turn to another diarist, John Evelyn. Despite the increased prosperity of the country since medieval times, the death rate among children was still appallingly high; only one in two could be expected to reach adulthood. John Evelyn and his wife suffered even worse than this, as poignant entries in his diary show. In 1654 they lost their second-born child, 'only a quarter old and as lovely a babe as ever I beheld'. Four years later their beloved firstborn died of fits: 'He was but five years and three days old, but even at that tender age, a prodigy for wit and understanding. . . . Here ends the joy of my life, for which I go mourning to the grave.' And then a fortnight later: 'The afflicting hand of God being still upon us, it pleased Him to take away from us this morning my other youngest son, George, now seven weeks languishing at nurse, breeding teeth and ending in a dropsy. God's

Childbirth for the high-born was a public, almost a social, affair, as this drawing of the birth of the Prince of Wales, James II's son, makes clear.

holy will be done.' Two more sons and three more daughters were born to the Evelyns, but one son died young and two daughters were carried off by smallpox in their teens. The remaining son reached the age of forty-four and produced an heir, but the only child of the large family to outlive Evelyn was his daughter Susanna. And they were a prosperous, enlightened family of country landowners; one wonders how any of the poor survived at all.

By the reign of the last Stuart monarch medicine still showed no apparent improvement, as the tragic story of Queen Anne herself proves. From seventeen pregnancies only one child survived, and he fell into a fever after the celebrations for his eleventh birthday. According to the fashion still prevailing he was bled and when a wiser physician, Dr Radcliffe, appeared it was too late: 'You have destroyed him and you may finish him,' he said, 'for I will not prescribe.' And so ended the Stuart line on the throne of England.

Doctor Radcliffe, in decrying bleeding as a cure-all, was well in advance of his time and unpopular. Bleeding was the common remedy for any complaint. If blood-letting from the finger was not effective they tried the toe or the ear; the theory was that bad blood was drawn off, to be replaced by a more benign fluid. The fact that blood circulated round the body had been proved by William Harvey, but that did not dispel the myth of good blood and bad. A method was devised of drawing off the blood with a fireproof, bell-shaped cup which, heated over a fire and thus filled with heat-expanded air, could be clapped on to the patient; as the air within it cooled, it contracted, to do by suction what must otherwise be done by knife.

Puritanism had not ended with the Restoration, and there was no lack of people who viewed with dismay and foreboding this new pleasure-loving, licentious society and prophesied that the wrath of God would fall upon them. It appeared to do so in the year 1665 in the form of the Great Plague, an epidemic comparable only to the Black Death of 1349. It struck most severely in London; some 70,000 people are believed to have died. Thousands fled from the city, business was at a standstill and grass grew in the streets. 'Little noise heard day or night but tolling of bells,' wrote Samuel Pepys.

In September 1666 the fire which James I had feared broke out in the city, in Pudding Lane. It burned for four days and nights and did incalculable damage. John Evelyn was a spectator:

The conflagration was so universal, and the people so astonished that from the beginning – I know not by what desponding or fate– they hardly stirred to quench it. There was nothing heard or seen but crying out and lamentation, and running about like distracted creatures without at all attempting to save even their goods. Such a strange consternation there was upon them that the fire burned, both in breadth and length, the churches, public halls, Exchange, hospitals, monuments and ornaments, leaping from house to house and street to street in a prodigious manner. . . . All the sky was of a fiery aspect like the top of a burning oven, and the light was seen for above forty miles round about for many nights. God grant my eyes may never behold the like, who now saw above ten thousand houses all in one flame.

The Great Fire destroyed nearly all of the old city of London but did not reach the slum areas outside. The central area benefitted therefore from the rebuilding with wider streets, tile or slate roofs instead of thatch, and brick, flat-fronted houses instead of the overhanging timber-framed houses of old London. And the genius of Sir Christopher Wren beautified the new city with lovely churches and the magnificent new St Paul's. But the slum areas were to remain as insanitary and overcrowded as they had been for centuries, and would remain so for another 200 years.

Out of the Great Fire came the beginnings of the fire service, but only for those who could afford it. A householder paid a stipulated sum annually and the symbol of the company which had insured him was prominently displayed on his house front. If fire broke out on insured premises the company's firemen would come, armed with leather buckets, grappling irons, and, later, small hand pumps. Uninsured houses were left to burn.

James II succeeded to the throne of his brother Charles II in 1685, but he was overthrown in the bloodless 'Glorious Revolution' of 1688 and his daughter Mary ruled jointly with her husband, William of Orange. William needed money for his wars and an unfortunate method of

OPPOSITE This engraving, dated 1690, shows a new fire engine being tested. It would presumably be less effective if there were no convenient high building from which to play the hose!

Day-bed, *c.* 1695, in
gilt wood and Genoa
velvet.

raising money was devised – a tax upon windows. It was stringent
considering the money value of the times: two shillings a window for
the first ten; four shillings for any further windows. The natural result
was that a good many windows were bricked up, but the tax raised
over a million pounds in the first year of its levying and was still a
source of revenue until the mid-nineteenth century. Many old houses
still have a window or two bricked up, some of them inside the glass.
Even more bear evidence that rooms designed as sleeping places for
servants had no windows at all, just a grating above the inner door to
admit a little light and air from a landing.

A happier result of the new reign was the Dutch influence on
gardens. The plan of the garden remained very formal but new plants

were introduced, particularly bulbs, in which the Dutch already specialized. A favourite flower they introduced was the hyacinth which had been bred from the wild bluebell. Other new plants came from much farther afield, for it was during this period that men began to make journeys with the sole purpose of discovering new plants. John Tradescant was one of these; he found a new rose in Russia, exceptionally sweet-scented, and from America he brought back a white daffodil as well as two familiar things which still bear the name of their place of origin – Virginia stock and Virginia creeper. And his own name is immortalized in the popular house plant, the tradescantia. Stay-at-home men also made their contribution; a clergyman in a village called Shirley in Surrey saw a white poppy growing among the red ones at the edge of a field. He transplanted it and by careful cultivation and cross-breeding produced the shirley poppy.

The influence of Dutch architecture resulted in the charming brick-built, flat-fronted, hipped-roofed houses of Queen Anne's reign. Great palaces like Blenheim were being built on a grandiose style, but the typical architecture of the age was the dignified symmetry of more modest houses like Tintinhull in Somerset or Mompesson House in the cathedral close at Salisbury. They heralded an age of unparalleled elegance and good taste in eighteenth-century England.

# 5 The Age of Elegance

he eighteenth century was an era of peace and security between the century of religious and political conflict and the century of industrialization. The dull Georges of the Hanoverian line sat securely on the throne while the Whigs and Tories argued eloquently in Parliament. A professional army fought wars abroad and there was little to distract the leisured classes from the enjoyment of beautiful homes, rich living, literature, music and art.

Their homes were mostly built in the simple Georgian style where beauty lay in firm adherence to the rules of proportion, which were laid down in the architects' manuals of the time. Isaac Ware expounded a golden rule in his *Complete Body of Architecture* in 1756.

Here is a space to be covered with building and the great consideration is its division into parts, for different uses; and their distribution. In this regard is to be had to two things, the convenience of the inhabitant, and the beauty and proportion of the fabric. Neither of these should be considered independently of the other. . . .

The style was particularly charming when applied to modest town houses, which were built of warm brick with tall sash windows exactly spaced, a small portico, perhaps, and a fanlight over the door. In large country houses elegance and proportion were sometimes put before practicality, despite Isaac Ware's advice. A central block contained the reception rooms but the stables and the kitchens would be in separate wings connected by a corridor or colonnade to the main building. At Holkham House, for example, built by William Kent for the Earl of Leicester in 1734, the kitchens were 200 feet from the dining-room. Some great houses, set in the centre of thousands of acres, were designed with basements which, though necessary in town houses, made nonsense in the country and must have been very unpleasant for the servants. The Italian architect Palladio was the inspiration of eighteenth-century architects and some houses suffered from being built too closely on models originally designed for the warmer climate of Italy: porticos in Italy helped to shield the house from the sun; in English Palladian villas such as Mereworth they cut off what little sun there was.

OPPOSITE An eighteenth-century family amuse themselves with music, books and toys. In an age when all but the poorest wore silk and lace, this was probably an ordinary middle-class family, with no pretensions to grandeur.

In the eighteenth century personal cleanliness began to assume more importance. These washstands are from one of Thomas Sheraton's pattern books. The holes on the top shelf held a bowl and other smaller vessels.

The great Georgian houses were richly decorated and furnished, though one wonders if they were not too elegant for comfort. Sir Thomas Robinson described Sir Robert Walpole's house at Houghton, built between 1722 and 1735 by Colen Campbell:

The furnishing of the inside is, I think, a pattern for all great houses that may hereafter be built: the vast quantities of mahogani, all the doors, window-shutters, best staircase, etc, being entirely of that wood; the finest chimnies of statuary and other fine marbles; the ceilings in the modern taste by Italians, painted by Mr Kent and finely gilt; the furniture of the richest tapestry etc, the paintings hung on Genoa velvet and damask. . . .

Mahogany was replacing oak as the major wood for decoration and furniture, though walnut enjoyed great popularity in the first half of the century. Furniture became much more graceful and makers like Hepplewhite, Chippendale and Sheraton developed their own particular styles. Inlay work became more fashionable than carving, and a variety of woods such as walnut, sycamore, boxwood and rosewood were used to give different shades and patterns.

Gardens were transformed from the middle of the century onwards when, as Horace Walpole said, William Kent 'leaped the fence, and saw all nature was a garden'. The lovely formal gardens which had endured since Tudor times were replaced by 'landscape' gardens which attempted to reproduce an idealized country scene. Even dead trees were occasionally planted to be true to nature. For posterity it was a sad thing that so many ancient gardens were destroyed, and some contemporaries did not favour the new fashion. Sir William Chambers complained that 'our gardens differ little from common fields' and imagined the unhappy experience of a stranger in a landscape garden:

At his first entrance he is treated with the sight of a large green field, scattered over with a few straggling trees, and verged with a confused border

The formal, geometric gardens of the seventeenth century were now replaced by gentle, sloping landscapes designed to enhance the house they surrounded. Humphrey Repton laid out these gardens at Sheffield Park, Sussex.

*The Josiah Wedgwood Family*, by Stubbs, dated 1780. Wedgwood was one of the early, benevolent industrialists, and cared deeply about the welfare of his pottery workers. Industrial conditions in the next century tended to be horrifyingly different.

of little shrubs and flowers; on further inspection he finds a little serpentine path, twining in regular esses amongst the shrubs of the border, upon which he is to go round, to look on one side at what he has already seen, the large green field, and on the other side at the boundary. . . . From time to time he perceives a little seat or temple stuck up against the wall: he rejoices at the discovery, sits down, rests his wearied limbs, and then reels on again, cursing the line of beauty; till, spent with fatigue, half roasted by the sun, for there is never any shade, and tired for want of entertainment he resolves to see no more: vain resolution! there is but one path, he must either drag on to the end or return by the tedious way he came.

While the houses of the rich became increasingly luxurious, the homes of the poor seem to have made little or no progress since

medieval times. In 1815, in the reign of the third George, R. W. Dickson surveyed the homes of 'poor farming peasants' in Lancashire. Some were well built in stone, roomy, and covered with slate or thatch, but many were still constructed in

A country family outside their cottage – watercolour by J. C. Ibbetson. Note the songbird in a cage above the cottage door.

a more ancient though less durable method . . . of forming them on wattled studwork with a composition of well-wrought loamy clay and cut straw. . . . These cottages have seldom more than a divided ground floor which with their brown sombre colour, gives them a hovel-like appearance far from agreeable and affords but little accommodation.

By 1825 the *Quarterly Review* was claiming that there had been great improvements in rural housing: 'It is now rare in the country to see a cottage without a brick or stone or wood floor, without stairs to the chambers, without plastering on the walls and without doors and windows tolerably weathertight.' Such very basic amenities seem hardly a cause for pride and indicate how bad things must have been in the previous century.

The meanest hovel, however, was preferable to the shelter of the workhouse to which the destitute were forced to go. Families were broken up, hours of work were long, food was scanty, discipline was inhumane. The chances of children surviving long enough to escape to a job were very slender. In 1760 Jonas Hanway revealed shocking mortality figures in *An Earnest Appeal for Mercy to the Children of the Poor*. In a certain parish:

of 54 children born, and taken into their workhouse, not one outlived the year in which it was born or taken in. This seemed to be so incredible, that I went to the workhouse to enquire into the fact and found it true. The workhouse was airy and well-situated but *such was their nursing*.

OPPOSITE Arthur Devis: *Sir George and Lady Strickland*. People would commission an artist to paint them in the same way that later generations would use photographers.

OVERLEAF *Mrs Congreve and Her Daughters in Their London Drawing-Room*. The uncluttered atmosphere of this room, with its simple, well-made Georgian furniture and plain marble fireplace, is in marked contrast to the claustrophobic interiors of Victorian times.

Despite his plea that 'Let the subject be ever so poor, humanity and religion do not change their nature' no humanity was introduced to the workhouses in his century or the next, as the novels of Dickens make clear. Two of the many rules of the Kendal workhouse in 1797 indicate why the prospect of the workhouse was a really terrifying one for the poor:

That no person be allowed to smoke in bed, or in their room, upon pain of being put six hours in the dungeon.

Persons convicted of lying, to be set on stools, in the most public place of the dining-room while the rest are at dinner, and have papers fixed on their breasts, with these words written thereon, INFAMOUS LYAR, and shall lose that meal.

The condition of the poorest classes, and of many small cultivators, suffered from the final wave of enclosures. As we have seen, enclosures had continued sporadically since medieval times, but there was a sudden and vast increase in the acreage enclosed when new methods of agriculture were introduced by men like Jethro Tull and Lord Townshend in the eighteenth century. The success of their methods

increased the profitability of land for the large farmer but demanded an amount of capital for machinery and fertilizer that the small farmer could not afford. Many yeoman farmers lost their independence and became tenants of landowners, or sold up their land and emigrated; the smallholder lost his rights to the common and probably his few acres too; the labourer was put out of work by the labour-saving machinery. So the landless and the unemployed drifted to the towns at the start of the great exodus which was to transform England from a rural to an urban society. Of course great profits were reaped from the agricultural revolution. More food was produced to feed the rising population; animals could be fed all through the winter so they no longer had to be killed each autumn; the release of labour to the towns enabled the growth of an industrialized society and, eventually, power and plenty to the working man. But no vision of affluent twentieth-century society cheered the countryman who found himself immured in a damp and smelly row of back-to-back houses in an eighteenth-century industrial town.

Another source of misery in the country was the decline of the domestic system of manufacture. In the past raw materials had been distributed to the cottages in a village and the finished work was collected from them. All the family shared in the work, as Daniel Defoe described in 1724:

Among the Manufacturer's Houses are likewise scattered an infinite Number of Cottages or small Dwellings, in which dwell the Workmen which are employed, the Woman and Children of whom are always busy Carding, Spinning etc so that no Hands being unemploy'd, all can gain their Bread, even from the youngest to the antient; hardly anything above four Years old, but its Hands are sufficient to it self.

As the century grew older the invention of powered machinery necessitated the setting up of factories, and women and children could no longer supplement the family income at home. It is sad to think of a four-year-old picking cotton all day, but even sadder to read of the experience of a boy in a silk mill in the middle of the century, working such long hours away from home that there can have been no family life at all.

OPPOSITE This was the really elegant side of eighteenth-century living – the State Bedroom at Nostell Priory, Yorkshire, with its magnificent plaster ceiling, gilt and marble fireplace, and eastern-inspired flowered wallpaper.

My parents, through mere necessity, put me to labour before Nature had
made me able. Low as the engines were, I was too short to reach them. To
remedy this defect, a pair of high pattens were fabricated and lashed to
my feet, which I dragged after me till time lengthened my stature. The
confinement and labour were no burden but the severity was intolerable, the
marks of which I yet carry and shall carry to my grave.

Many of the people who, because of the enclosures or for other reasons
sought work in industry, were those who had been used to growing
their own vegetables. The woman of the house, even when casually or
seasonally employed, had always tended her garden or her bit of
common land and cooked what it produced. In the towns more and
more frequently the man of the family could not earn enough for all, so
his wife went on to the labour market too and had neither the time nor,
in the horrible, hastily erected houses, the facilities for cooking. Whole

families became dependent upon bought food. Somebody discovered
that any greenstuff from cabbages to pickles took on an enhanced
colour if boiled in a copper pan with a little vinegar; people who bought
such stuff were buying poison in the form of copper sulphate. Some
very strange things went into bread and into tea, and one way of
making poor, weak beer develop a good head of froth was to add the
sudsy water in which linen had been washed. Butter and cheese were
artificially coloured, milk watered down, and in spite of the Anglo-
Saxon prejudice against eating horseflesh, which only extreme famine
could lift, who knows what went into the meat pies sold at every
cookshop? Folklore often embodies a truth – what of Sweeney Todd?

Even the wealthy in towns of any size drank dubious milk. Milk
soured quickly, especially in warm weather, and transport by horse
quickened the process; so the cow must be brought nearer to the
customer. In a sense factory farming had begun. A newly calved cow
would be brought into a cowshed, necessarily crowded, and often
indeed underground. She never saw green grass again; she was fed,
often on bad hay and the remnants of grain after the brewers had
malted it. She stood hock-deep in filth and lived in an appalling stench
until she ceased to give milk. Then she went to the butcher's shambles.

A few cows were more fortunate; they grazed in St James' Park and
usually their customers came to them, drinking milk on the spot. That
at least ensured that it had not been watered down. Another source of
milk, considered to be good for children and invalids, was the donkey.
There again blind instinct or the accumulated knowledge of the ages
was at work. The donkey did not harbour the germs of bovine
tuberculosis. It was no rare thing to see a she-ass being milked in a
fashionable street with sedan chairs and carriages coming and going in
the background.

It is perhaps arguable that sugar was partly responsible for the fact
that teeth now needed special attention, but it may not have been the
only culprit, for in the Sugar Islands themselves, where people went
about sucking and chewing sugar cane, teeth were generally good. The
refining of sugar, and of food generally, may have had an adverse effect
upon teeth. It is noticeable that primitive people usually have enviable
teeth. Some people – not dentists, for the trade was not specialized in

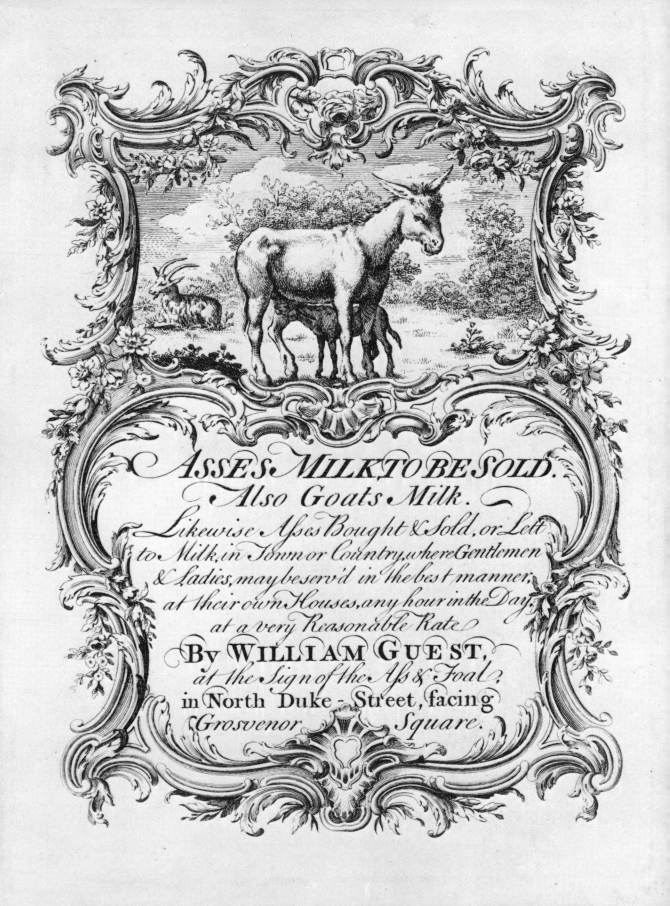

ASSES MILK, TO BE SOLD.
Also Goats Milk.
Likewise Asses Bought & Sold, or Lett
to Milk, in Town or Country, where Gentlemen
& Ladies, may be serv'd in the best manner,
at their own Houses, any hour in the Day,
at a very Reasonable Rate
By WILLIAM GUEST,
at the Sign of the Ass & Foal,
in North Duke-Street, facing
Grosvenor Square.

This was an age when all but the poorest had at least one servant. Hogarth's painting entitled *Heads of Six of Hogarth's Servants* reveals their personalities with the accuracy of a camera lens.

the eighteenth century – blamed the use of toothpicks which, they said, chipped the enamel. (Yet some savage tribes habitually file their teeth into points without detriment to anything but their appearance.) And if it was important to preserve the enamel on the outside of teeth, some of the tooth powders and pastes just coming into use could hardly have assisted this aim; chalk and salt were harmless enough, but powdered pumice mixed to a paste with soap was also in common use. Such preparations, somebody said, should not be called tooth polishers but gum bleeders.

Soon there were sufficient aching teeth defying the homely remedies to justify people setting up as tooth-pullers. A strong wrist and a pair of pliers were all that was needed. The praise lavished on those who could extract a tooth at the first pull is dismal comment. The tooth-puller moved from market to market, and from fair to fair, often accompanied by a boy with a drum which he banged first to attract a crowd and then to drown the screams of the poor victims. For the crowd a tooth-pulling provided entertainment; most people in the eighteenth century were indifferent to the sufferings of others – even the elegant world regarded a visit to Bedlam to see lunatics flogged as a pleasant afternoon's outing.

The vain and rich had one chance, though it was a slim one, of escaping the disfigurement of a gap-toothed jaw. A healthy tooth could be bought from a young person anxious to earn a shilling. Then, with the patient rendered slightly insensitive by brandy or laudanum, the tooth would be extracted. The bespoken healthy tooth was then drawn from the other jaw and transferred. Some of these early transplants were successful, but most failed, being rejected as the gum healed. Even then all was not lost. Another sound tooth could be bought and fitted with little gold hooks which would secure it to the teeth on either side of the gap. Naturally such operations were conducted in private. A really far-sighted person, aware of a hole in a tooth which might lead to toothache later, could have a filling of wax or plaster or gold according to his means; but since the hole was merely filled, and the decay was not first drilled out as in modern dentistry, the rotting process went on behind the stopping.

Reading the *Compleat City and Country Cook*, published in 1736, it appears that medical knowledge was still enveloped in superstition and tradition. Alongside recipes for such delicacies as 'Sparrow Pye' are cures for common ailments such as 'Rednys and Shining of the Nose' and thinning hair. Washing in dew collected on a May morning was supposed to cure a luminous nose and an ointment made of bear's grease, ashes, almond oil and the juice of a lily root would make hair grow if applied 'the day before the full of the moon'. The most revolting cure is the one offered 'For Spitting of Blood if a Vein is broken':

Take the Dung of Mice, beat it to Powder, put as much as will lie upon a sixpence in a quarter of a pint of juice of Plantane, and sweeten with a little sugar. Give it in a morning fasting and at night going to Bed. Continue this for sometime and it will complete the cure.

However, medicine did make one great advance in the last quarter of the eighteenth century. Edward Jenner is given the credit of first advocating vaccination against smallpox. He, like many before him, had noticed that cows often had pustules on their udders, and that milkmaids caught a relatively mild disease called cow-pox. Such people seemed to be immune to the deadly smallpox, and milkmaids' complexions, being unpitted, were much admired. Jenner argued that to woo cow-pox by scratching a healthy skin and rubbing into it some of the matter taken from a cow-pox sore would guard against small-pox. He made his theory public in 1776, but he had in fact been forestalled by a Devon farmer, Benjamin Jesty, who had vaccinated his wife and two sons two years earlier. What became of the sons is not recorded, but his wife lived on for another forty years. Vaccination became a matter of great controversy. There were some mishaps; no operation at the time was performed in sterile conditions, and the merest scratch could become infected. There was another risk in that the cow, or the person from whom the cow-pox matter was taken, might unknowingly be suffering from some other complaint which would then be transferred. Enlightened people were willing to take the risk both for themselves and their children, and the custom gradually grew so that smallpox ceased to be a scourge.

Other killers beside smallpox stalked the streets. One of them was gin – but not the pure, clean spirit that we know. Some miserable people drank terrible concoctions of sulphuric acid thinly disguised by the addition of sugar, a little rose water, or a dribble of lime juice. It was the drink of the poor and the wretched – social prejudice against it lasted well into the twentieth century and is not yet quite dead. For people in the eighteenth century, many of them country people who had been forced to seek work in towns, who were exploited by their employers, whose homes were far worse than a clod cottage and more overcrowded, a glass of gin offered a form of escapism. And one glass led to another, and another. . . .

OPPOSITE Hogarth's horrific engraving of *Gin Lane* shows the destructiveness of this social evil in every detail.

Hogarth was a brilliant and merciless exposer of people and their weaknesses, and certainly domestic bliss was not found behind every Georgian front door. His painting *Marriage à la Mode*, executed in 1745, depicts a dejected and disillusioned young husband with his extravagant wife.

Tea was an expensive luxury when first imported into Britain. In this painting, *A Family at Tea*, attributed to R. Coins and dated *c.* 1730, tea is being drunk not from cups but from handle-less dishes.

A licence was needed to sell ale or beer, but anybody could sell gin. In the worst London slums every fifth house was at one time a gin shop. And the home-made concoction which had paid no duty was cheap. Some places advertised 'Drunk for a penny; dead drunk for twopence; straw for nothing.' The straw was in the shed or outhouse where the dead drunk could lie while recovering from whatever poison in the name of gin they had imbibed. The problem grew so great that Parliament was stirred to action and in 1751 the Gin Act increased duties on the spirit and forbade its sale by distillers and retailers. The

reason given was that 'the moderate drinking of distilled spiritous liquors by persons of the meanest and lowest sort, hath of late years increased, to the great detriment of the health and morals of the common people.' The Act was successful in greatly reducing deaths through drink, but the problems of drunkenness in cities remained severe until late in the next century.

Drunkenness was not confined to the 'lowest sort'. The eighteenth century was a time of excessive drinking among the upper classes, too, when it was quite common for male guests to drink themselves into

*View of a Drawing-Room,* by an unknown artist, dated 1780. A pleasant interior, with a woman sewing. The gilt chairs are clearly French-influenced. By now tea is being drunk from cups, not dishes.

a stupor and have to be carried out to their conveyance by their servants. Gambling was another vice of the upper classes. It was so highly regarded that men risked bankruptcy rather than admit the stakes were too high for them. When James Boswell came to London he was relieved that his promise to Sheridan not to play for five years prevented him ruining himself, though at the same time he admitted feeling at a disadvantage 'as people get acquainted much easier when set round a card table'.

Happy it is for me that I am thus tied up; for with my warmth and impetuosity of temper, I might go to the greatest lengths and soon involve myself in ruin and misery. There is no setting bounds to gaming when one engages keenly in it; and it is more genteel to say you never play than to refuse playing for whatever sums the company choose.

One gentleman of title, having staked and lost all he possessed, offered his wife as forfeit in the next game. He lost. Fortunately she was one of the few women of the period with resources of her own; next day she went to the man who had won her, paid him what she had been considered worth overnight and bought herself free. There is, alas, no record of the subsequent relations between husband and wife. An eminent statesman, rising from a table at which he had lost £5,000 in an evening, remarked that it was a good thing that he was not playing deep. Gambling sessions could last all night, and because no player wanted to miss a single moment, the cupboards of the elegant, now much sought after Georgian sideboards were provided with chamber pots. This custom, like the gin shop, belongs to the reverse side of what is often known as the Age of Elegance.

Eighteenth-century fashion was also unworthy of the architecture, art, music and literature of the period. It was distinguished by ornateness and artificiality which reached a peak of absurdity in the hair fashions in the third quarter of the century. Women's hair and men's wigs were greased and pomaded and then heavily powdered white. Small rooms or large cupboards were reserved for powdering so that bedchambers should not be messed up. Women's hair was dressed high in front, with ringlets falling at the back, and fantastic ornaments, often made of spun glass, were attached to the high-piled hair. There was competition in originality and in extremity; the lady who carried a whole battle scene on her head scored slightly over the one who had a mere coach and horses; the one who was content with a few butterflies was plainly a non-starter. The decorations could be removed at bedtime, but the elaborate coiffure itself was disturbed as little as possible. The truly fashionable lady slept in strange postures sometimes with her neck in a hollowed-out log leaving her head clear. It might be several days, or even weeks, before the hairdo was, as they termed it, 'opened up'. It is sad to think that the elegant lady of the portraits and the porcelain figurines was lousy, but she could hardly fail to be.

The French Revolution encouraged the return to nature, but nature in classical style. Away with the corsets, the steel hoops that held skirts wider than they had ever been; away with the wig; away, too, with sumptuousness in clothing – muslin or plain silk complemented the new silhouette better. Women's hair was dressed simply, and held with ribbon in a style vaguely reminiscent of Ancient Greece, or even cut short and if necessary curled. The straight gown was girdled, just below the bosom, and worn over a single petticoat which rash young women wore damp so that it clung to the figure and emphasized the statuesque, classical outline. Men, one imagines, abandoned their wigs with pleasure. They had been reducing them all through the century and the wig which went out with the new fashion for simplicity was the kind now worn by barristers in court. For men of the late eighteenth century the two greatest changes were the abandonment of silk and satin and bright colours and the move from breeches to trousers.

The reaction against ornate dress originated in France. In England it was stimulated by George Brummell – Beau Brummell – whose life story proves that rigid as class distinctions in the eighteenth century may seem to us, they were far less rigid than in any other European country. He was the grandson of a valet who left service and opened an apartment house, where he did so well that his grandson went to Eton, no longer a school for poor boys as it had been at its foundation, and then to Oxford. Brummell became an intimate friend of the Prince of Wales, presently to be Regent and then King, and his influence grew so great that he became the prime arbiter of fashion. He thought men's

The excesses of fashion have always made some laugh, while others slavishly follow them, however ridiculous.

RIGHT The height of the hair was only matched by the width of the skirt. Such complicated constructions were rarely 'opened up', and would have become quite verminous.

BELOW William Hogarth: *The Staymaker*. To achieve this kind of outline the stays must have been very hard, very tight and very uncomfortable . . . but one must suffer to be beautiful.

OPPOSITE Vanity was by no means restricted to women. A Regency dandy admires himself in his mirror before sallying forth, hopefully, no doubt, to be admired by others.

clothes should be plain, but well-cut; and that cleanliness of person and body linen should be of paramount importance. The Prince of Wales was so thoroughly converted to Brummell's views that one of the many reasons he gave for not getting along with the wife chosen for him was that she lacked fastidiousness in such matters.

The fixed bath, in a permanent bathroom, was still a great rarity. There was one in the Pavilion at Brighton, but since it was enormous, and used seawater, it was hardly a domestic installation. Even when Buckingham House became Buckingham Palace it had no bathroom. The portable bath, round or oval, placed in winter before a good fire and filled and emptied by servants, was still thought to be satisfactory. More and more people, however, were enjoying an occasional total immersion; at Bath, where the medicinal qualities of the water had been recognized by the Romans, or at the seaside. Fanny Burney described her mixed feelings on first using a bathing machine in 1773. At first she was 'terribly frightened' but when she had recovered from the shock of the plunge 'I presently felt myself in a glow that was delightful – it is the finest feeling in the world, and will induce me to bathe as often as will be safe.' Doctors were divided in their opinion of this hydromania; some advising bathing, especially for children and those inclined to be delicate, others deploring it and foretelling woe in the form of rheumatism and lung disorders. The Duke of Wellington, however, took a cold bath every morning, and lived to be eighty.

Indoor sanitation made a move forward in 1775, when a watchmaker named Alexander Cummings took out a patent for a water closet with a U-bend behind the bowl so that, after flushing, a certain amount of water stayed there to prevent the blow-back of poisonous sewer gas which had made earlier installations so dangerous. He named his invention for what it was – a 'water closet' – and in many places far from England the letters WC are his memorial. The pans and overhead cisterns were made in pottery, and some were splendidly decorated; the rest of the work went to plumbers and cabinet makers. One cabinet maker, Joseph Brahmah, in fitting out WCs to Cummings' design, felt he could improve on the original, and did so with such success that his design remained unchallenged for well over a hundred years, and some Brahmah closets are still in use today. That there was a demand for such an amenity is proved by the fact that Brahmah claimed he had set up 6000 WCs within nine years of taking out his patent. His closet was still something for the well-to-do, of course, and the attitude towards what happened after the flushing process remained dangerously careless; it took the cholera epidemics of the next century to make people think seriously about drains and sewers.

Plans for houses of any quality made after 1775 generally allowed space for the WC. In older houses they were pushed in anywhere, often under the stairs. The wood used for the seat was almost invariably mahogany and it is interesting to think that mahogany had thus come full circle, since its first known use had been purely utilitarian. During a voyage to the New World, a carpenter on one of Sir Walter Raleigh's ships had been forced to make a repair with what wood was available, and he praised the local mahogany for its hardness, its durability and its beauty.

Another new amenity, at first restricted in use by its cost, was a simple, quick way of kindling a flame – the forerunner of the match as we know it. All one needed was a splinter of wood, tipped with sulphur, and a fold of coarse paper coated with phosphorus – a substance discovered by a seventeenth-century alchemist still on the ancient quest for a method of turning base metal into gold.

The invention which most affected the ordinary housewife, however, was the kitchen range designed by Thomas Robinson in 1780. The fire was closed-in with an oven on one side and a tank for heating water on the other. Since food could be boiled or fried on top of the stove, one fire thus performed three functions – or even four, for when the opening at the top of the stove was closed, the rack above made a safe place for airing clothes. This enabled families to make a great saving on fuel. The method of cooking by pot above, or spit before, an open hearth was wasteful; much of the heat went up the chimney or dispersed itself about the kitchen. In a range the heat was confined and, by means of the dampers in the flue that led to the chimney, controllable. The invention was particularly welcome in towns where all fuel had to be bought and was very expensive until the digging of the canal system cheapened the cost of transport. The range had one drawback – it stood low, with only a plinth of stone or brickwork separating it from the

Inventions are rarely accepted overnight. Rowlandson's watercolour of the *Inside of a Kitchen at Newcastle*, printed and published in 1800, still shows an open fire, rather than the more modern kitchen range, being used for cooking. The spit is powered by the little dog paddling away in the treadmill contraption on the wall.

floor, so a great deal of stooping and lifting was required which the spit and the brick oven did not demand. The resultant backaches went unnoticed and it is only very recently, in the most up to date kitchens, that ovens have been set higher.

On an old hearth which has never been closed in, or on one recently exposed by conversion, it is possible to stoop and look up through a wide vertical passage to the sky. Often these chimneys are ridged inside, and a lively child would not find climbing it too great a hardship. But in the eighteenth century houses in towns were being built with an eye to space-saving; the much admired terraces in London, Bath and Brighton are the result of the trend to build high rather than wide. Chimneys were proportionately narrowed and heightened, and to climb one, scrabbling the soot away with one's hands and feet, was a daunting task. Only a small boy could manage it, and there were plenty of them about; they too, could be obtained from workhouses, or bought for a negligible sum from a desperate or callous parent. There are accounts of little boys who got stuck in chimneys and died, and of fires being lighted under them to make them climb faster. Apart from this, they often developed cancer as the result of flesh scraped raw coming into contact with soot. Even in the nineteenth century, when the use of boy sweeps was made illegal, and the invention of brushes made them unnecessary, it took many years, and many prosecutions, before the practice was at last stamped out.

In the late eighteenth century there developed through satirical writings and cartoons the figure of an apocryphal typical Englishman, John Bull. The balance of power was beginning to shift from agriculture to industry, but observers of the time still saw the bluff, stout-hearted but rather stupid and narrow-minded country gentleman as typical of the nation. John Bull was a farmer. He either owned his land, or was such a good tenant that his tenure was certain; politically and religiously he was sound – Tory and Church of England. And if the rhyme on the mug from which he drank his ale was even half true, he was unique – a happy man, contented with his lot.

> Let the wealthy and great
> Roll in splendour and state,
> I envy them not, I declare it.
> I eat my own lamb,
> My own chicken and ham,
> I shear my own fleece and I wear it.
> I have lawns, I have bowers,
> I have fruits, I have flowers,
> The lark is my morning alarmer.
> So jolly boys now,
> Here's God speed the plough!
> Long life and success to the farmer!

He may not have been completely typical, but typical enough to be taken seriously; and so was his wife – George Eliot's Mrs Poyser *must* have been drawn from life. She was busy in kitchen and dairy, and quite grand in her parlour which might even include amongst its furnishings a spinet, the mother of the piano, or as the making of

*An Elegant Establishment for Young Ladies* by E. F. Burney. Parents could not always be sure their daughters were acquiring the right sort of education!

pianos became a business, a piano itself. John Bull could afford to keep a gig, though the tax was heavy – £6 a year; he could also afford to educate some of his children. Education for the eldest son could be sketchy – a year or two at the nearest Grammar School, or with a parson who needed to supplement his meagre living by taking pupils; younger sons needed more education, for they had to make their own way in the world. John Bull stuck to the feudal rule of primogeniture.

In France, or so he heard, holdings of land were equally divided between all a man's progeny so that each generation owned individually less and less. And look what had happened there! John Bull wanted nothing to do with anything French. His daughters went to the Female Academies which were proliferating rapidly: they were places where girls were taught well or badly according to the quality of those in charge, but at least acquired a smattering of basic learning and a few trimmings such as music, dancing, deportment and painting.

John Bull is always depicted wearing a Union Jack waistcoat; otherwise his dress is that of any prosperous eighteenth-century countryman – riding clothes consisting of breeches and boots, cutaway coat, and the low top hat which was the horseman's crash helmet. He is often accompanied by his counterpart in the canine world – the bulldog. Brutal sports were still acceptable to all but the minority, and the bulldog had been specially bred for bull-baiting. His prognathous jaw gave him a good hold and his recessed nostrils enabled him to breathe while that hold was maintained. He became the symbol of tenacity.

Roast meat was still the basic diet of town and country gentlemen, as the Swedish professor Peter Kalm noted rather disparagingly during his visit in 1748. The English were good at roasting, he said, 'which is not to be wondered at because the art of cooking as practised by most Englishmen does not extend much beyond roast beef and plum pudding'. However, he enjoyed the new experience of eating toast for breakfast: '. . . they ate at the same time, one or more slices of wheatbread which they had first roasted by the fire, and when it was very hot, had spread butter on it, and then placed it a little way from the fire that the butter might melt well into the bread.'

Peter Kalm was very struck by the apparent idleness of women compared with those of his native Sweden. 'England is a paradise for ladies and women', he said, and continued:

They never take the trouble to bake, because there is a baker in every parish or village, from whom they can always have new bread. Nearly the same can be said about brewing. Weaving and spinning is also in most houses a more than rare thing, because their many manufacturers save them from the necessity of such.

Differences in class and income in early nineteenth-century London are sharply contrasted here.

ABOVE A well-stocked game and poultry stall, with well-dressed customers.

RIGHT A print entitled 'Fat and Lean or feeding the hungry' – the customers have little to spend, their money is considered suspect, and paper to wrap their meagre purchases is refused them.

While the availability of manufactured goods, for the classes who could afford them, undoubtedly relieved some of the labour of housekeeping, idleness was to become a cultivated affectation by the end of the century. A 'lady' was no longer allowed to soil her hands in household tasks. A fleet of servants carried out her orders while she passed the day in the dreary round of visiting and receiving, embroidery and letter-writing which is portrayed in the novels of Jane Austen at the turn of the century. Women had always occupied a subordinate role, but it had been a full and energetic one even among the upper classes. Now they were to be relegated to the position of weak and submissive playthings, in, ironically, the reign of a vigorous and assertive Queen.

# 6 Poverty and Affluence

he young Princess Victoria, roused from her bed early on a June morning in 1837 and informed that she was Queen of England, said, 'I will be good.' Nobody would dispute the fact that she was good, if wilful, and headstrong and egocentric in the true Hanoverian fashion. She was fortunate enough to fall in love with and to marry an extremely virtuous, earnest, puritanical young German – Albert the Good. Together they set up the pattern of English domestic family life, but with two faces – one, the ideal family, making its own entertainment, singing around the piano, playing charades or word games; the other darker, a masculine-dominated enclave with Papa the unchallenged dictator. Victorian novels reflect this contrast in styles of family life: Dickens describes the cruelty of David Copperfield's stepfather and of Dombey to his daughter but also paints many idyllic pictures of domestic happiness, such as the Cratchits' Christmas dinner.

Victoria and Albert had nine children and this was not unusual for the times; more children were surviving because of medical improvements. Like most of her female subjects Queen Victoria dreaded childbirth which she called 'the shadow-side of marriage'. It was not only the pain she feared but the 'complete violence to all one's feelings of propriety'. In 1858 she wrote with realism to her daughter the Princess Royal during her first pregnancy: 'What you say of the pride of giving life to an immortal soul is very fine, dear, but I own I cannot enter into that; I think much more of our being like a cow or a dog at such moments; when our poor nature becomes so very animal & unecstatic. . . .' Five years earlier the Queen had first experienced 'that blessed Chloroform' during the birth of her eighth child. She found it 'soothing, quieting, and delightful beyond measure', and for those who could afford chloroform childbirth and operations lost some of their terror. In 1860 Lister introduced antiseptic surgery, and though it was greeted with disbelief the consequent reduction in mortality soon proved his point.

In middle- and upper-class families most of the children so painfully brought into the world saw little of their parents during their childhood. Most of their life was spent in the seclusion of the nursery

OPPOSITE The worst aspects of Victorian industrialization are evident in Doré's brilliant engraving of back-to-backs in London. The railway arch seems to dominate the houses in the same way that the rich dominated the poor.

TO THE
QUEEN'S PRIVATE APARTMENTS

THE QUEEN AND PRINCE ALBERT AT HOME.

from which they would be summoned at their cleanest and neatest to join their parents for a short period each day. Boys were taught by tutors until they were old enough to be sent away to barbaric public schools. Girls often had governesses until they exchanged the school-room for the drawing-room, but a few were sent to young ladies' academies where they acquired little education but many accomplishments. The Taunton Report on Endowed Schools in 1867 regretted the prevailing belief:

that girls are less capable of mental cultivation and less in need of it than boys; that accomplishments and what is showy and superficially attractive, are what is really essential for them; and in particular, as regards their relationship with the other sex, and the probabilities of marriage, more solid attainments are actually disadvantageous rather than the reverse.

The cruel discipline and bullying which many boys suffered at their public schools was not always escaped by their sisters left at home. Exact obedience was expected from Victorian children and any departure from this was punished severely. In 1869 the *Saturday Review* commented with distaste on the relish with which many mothers flogged their daughters; the article was occasioned by a six months' exchange of methods of flogging which had appeared in the letter columns of the *Englishwoman's Domestic Magazine*:

That in the year 1869, there should be living in England and in London, a considerable number of women, many apparently in good society, and some of them titled, who are in the regular habit of stripping and flogging with birches, apple-twigs, or leather straps, their daughters of thirteen years old and upward, must appear to foreigners incredible, and to most Englishmen very queer. . . . They seem to glory in the privilege of thrashing their girls.

Such cruelty seems particularly astonishing, as do other unpleasant aspects of Victorian England, in a society which throbbed with honest religious fervour. Family prayers were at least a daily occurrence in the classes which had time for them, and strict religious principles turned Sundays into a day which Victorian children dreaded. In 1905 Samuel Smiles looked back at his childhood in his autobiography:

Sunday 'the day of rest' was to us the most exhausting and unpleasant of

OPPOSITE To many people Victoria and Albert and their numerous children were the ideal family. Frictions certainly arose later when the children grew up, but they look happy enough here romping in the royal nursery with Prince Albert.

the week. . . . We had no sort of recreation on Sundays. Walking, except to the kirk, was forbidden. Books were interdicted, excepting the Bible, the Catechism, and the Secession Magazine, or perhaps some book of Evangelical sermons. I have no doubt it was all intended for our good; but I never in my youth had any agreeable recollection of Sundays.

Even very young children were forced to sit quietly and do nothing all day except perhaps listen to improving reading and, of course, go to church. A rhyme in the *Infants Magazine* in 1868 tells of the sad locking away of toys on a Saturday night:

> Haste! put your playthings all away,
> To-morrow is the sabbath-day;
> Come bring to me your Noah's Ark,
> Your pretty, tinkling music cart;
> Because, my love, you must not play,
> But holy keep the sabbath-day.

In some fortunate families a Noah's Ark was permitted because of its religious association!

Victorian children in the middle and upper classes grew up in homes ranging from the elegant terraces in Knightsbridge to large Gothic mansions ornamented with turrets and battlements in the rage for the medieval and the romantic. Many of the more modest Victorian houses have a spaciousness and a decorative detail which is enviable compared with the tightly packed boxes of modern times, but the rich built with a tastelessness previously unknown to British architecture. Lovely Georgian houses were pulled down to make way for mock-Tudor mansions and Tudor houses were demolished to build neo-Gothic castles.

The interiors of Victorian houses were heavily and often oppressively ornamented. Everything that could be decorated was decorated, and anything that could be made to look other than it was, was so disguised. The beautiful classical fireplaces of the former century were either ripped out or hidden by draperies of velvet or plush, heavily bobbled; the piano must be draped for it had legs and now legs were supposedly non-existent (and trousers, if they must be referred to at all, were called unmentionables). So small a thing as a

thimble must have its little case; a boiled egg could not come to table as a boiled egg – it must nestle in a dish, under a lid moulded and coloured into a life-like model of a nesting hen. The ordinary sitting-room of the time must have been a housemaid's nightmare. Photographs exist of these cluttered places, for the photographic process was developed in the first half of the century. Soon, among the wax flowers, the stuffed birds, the dried flowers, all under glass domes, stood the photographs of dear ones, living and dead.

It was Victoria who set the fashion for the extraordinary mourning cult which swept the country. Albert died in 1861, when Victoria was only forty-two, and all the passionate adoration which had surrounded the living Albert was transformed into passionate reverence for the dead. Victoria remained in widow's weeds for the next thirty years. A

Any feeling of spaciousness in a Victorian room was quickly dispelled by the vast quantities of solid furniture, heavy draperies and potted palms without which no self-respecting Victorian family felt at home.

OPPOSITE ABOVE
George Lance:
*Preparation for a
Banquet*. An early
Victorian painting of
the kitchen of a
wealthy house.

OPPOSITE BELOW
An anonymous
painting of a cricket
match at
Christchurch,
Hampshire, *c*. 1850.
The women in the
crowd are wearing
crinolines and poke
bonnets, and carrying
parasols.

OVERLEAF The
seaside and sea
bathing had started
to become fashionable
in Regency times, and
by the mid-
nineteenth century
the idea was firmly
established. However,
clothing and furniture
were ill adapted to
beach life, as this
painting entitled *A
Day by the Seaside*
shows.

distinguishing dress for widows had first been devised in the eighteenth century; it was black and white, and not at all unbecoming. The Georgians were somewhat disposed to take death lightly – a skull, properly mounted, made a good paperweight. Victorian mourning was a serious business and followed strict rules. Yards and yards of black crepe draped the widow from head to heel, black-edged announcements of deaths appeared in papers, the bereaved used black-edged writing paper and black-edged handkerchiefs, and men wore bands of black crepe around their hats or on their sleeves. The *Home Book*, published in the 1870s, described the procedure to be followed 'upon the occasion of a death in the family':

The first sign to the outer world that one of a certain home circle is 'smitten by the common stroke of death' is the closing of the blinds at the windows of the house and the non-appearance in public of the female members of the family. The next step . . . is the ordering of the coffin, sending notes to all relations and particular friends apprising them of the mournful intelligence, and despatching obituary notices to the newspapers. . . . Ladies if chief mourners wear dresses made of stuff and crape only, and gentlemen black suits and neckties, a crape scarf worn across one shoulder and crape hatband. Those not related to the deceased wear black with moderate-sized hatband and black gloves.

Some Victorians, however, viewed the ostentatious cult of grief with distaste. Dickens insisted in his will that he should be buried in 'an inexpensive, unostentatious, and strictly private manner' and asked the mourners to 'wear no scarf, cloak, black bow, long hat-band or other absurdity'. But the poor, unfortunately, attached great importance to a respectable funeral and many saved pence they could ill afford to ensure they did not suffer a pauper's burial.

Men who were bereaved of their wives were allowed, indeed expected, to revive and remarry. Widows were not; full mourning and total social isolation were the rule for at least a year and then half-mourning, in purple or mauve. From then on all interest was expected to be concentrated upon the family, or upon good works. Behind the sombre dress and the social retirement of widows an unrecognized, subconscious force may have been at work. The marriage market was already overcrowded with females. Much Victorian literature shows

how deeply preoccupied parents were with the problem of finding husbands for their daughters. Possibly always, and certainly since records have been kept, the number of male births has slightly exceeded that of females, but more boys died young. This imbalance was increased by war and by the drainage of eligible young men to administer the colonies of the Empire. A few women, determined to marry, went out to Asia and Africa where white women were at a premium, but the majority stayed at home and engaged in desperate competition for husbands while their youth lasted, which in Victorian times was not very long. The epithets, 'old maid', 'spinster', 'on the shelf', began to haunt the average young woman who reached the middle twenties without finding a mate. For her the future was bleak. In the eyes of the world, and of her parents, she was a failure, doomed to stay at home, gradually taking over the housekeeping as her mother aged and all too often ending up as aunt to her brother's family, or her married sister's. It is not by accident that an agency, set up in the twentieth century, and offering almost every kind of useful service that women could supply, should call itself Universal Aunts.

It is saddening to think of all the talent and energy frittered away in those claustrophobic homes. The very few women who managed to break away did so well under such severe handicaps. Florence Nightingale revolutionized hospitals; Dorothea Beale and Frances Buss laid the foundations of higher education for women; Elizabeth Fry devoted her life to prison and social reform; and Mrs Samuel Baker in her hampering Victorian clothes braved the tropical heat of the Sudan in the search for the source of the Nile. These women were exceptional, not so much in themselves, as in their circumstances. Hundreds, equally able, were doomed to inaction. Some took refuge in ill-health. Of this escape mechanism Elizabeth Barrett Browning is a classic example. Her father may not have been quite the ogre depicted by Charles Laughton on the cinema screen, but he was, give or take a little, almost typical. Elizabeth suffered a slight accident in youth and then took to her sofa. She lay on it, or in her bed, for thirty years, enveloped in the domineering affection of a stern father. Luckier than most, she had creative ability, and her poems attracted the attention of another poet, Robert Browning. Inspired by him, she found

OPPOSITE ABOVE
F. D. Hardy: *The First Birthday Party*, 1867. A wealth of domestic detail can be discerned in this cottage interior – of particular interest are the clay pipe and the cup and ball toy on the floor, the wooden sewing box on the mantelpiece, and the heavy flat iron on the table by the window.

OPPOSITE BELOW
R. Martineau: *The Last Day in the Old Home*. A poignant scene – debts have caused the break-up of family life and the house has to be sold. Clearly there is a sharp division between father and son on the one hand, and mother and daughter on the other.

Sentimental or
appealing, depending
on one's attitude,
Prince Albert
certainly brought a
lot of excitement into
children's lives by
introducing the
Christmas tree from
his native Germany.

strength enough to leave her sofa, make a runaway marriage at the age of forty, go to Italy, bear a child, and live another fifteen years.

However, not all the swoons and cries for smelling salts were of psychological origin. Tight lacing, the fiercest ever known, was back in fashion. 'Strait-laced' as applied to a person, an age, or a society, is no idle term. The young Victorian girl, hoping for marriage, conformed to fashion. An eighteen-year-old was allowed a waist measurement of eighteen inches; at nineteen another inch was permitted, and at twenty another. That was the limit. The smallness of the waist was emphasized by enormously wide skirts and deep lace collars, called berthes, which fell from the neckline. For evening wear this was cut both low and wide, so that many dresses appeared to be slipping off the shoulders. Sloping shoulders were desired and all fashionable women seemed to attain the ideal, or to give an illusion of it. The emphasis for the unmarried was on youth: simplicity, innocence, demureness. Hair was parted in the centre and allowed to fall in ringlets on either side of the face (rather like a spaniel's ears), or smoothly brushed, covering the ears on either side, then caught in a heavy chignon at the nape of the neck. The young wore few jewels since a string of pearls suited the innocent look best, and there was a pleasing fashion for a little posy of real flowers pinned to the berthe. White and pale pastel colours were in vogue for the young. Innocence was more than genuine enough; many girls went to the marriage bed in total ignorance of the facts of life.

After marriage the emphasis changed to staidness and dignity; a married woman could wear stronger colours, richer fabrics, more jewellery. Cameos were very fashionable. When in mourning – and with such large families and with so much attention focused on grief, most women were in mourning for much of the time – jet could be worn, and any ornament either made of or incorporating some of the dead person's hair. Lockets which opened to show a tiny photograph of the mourned one on one side, and a wisp of hair on the other, were to be found in every woman's jewel box. One did not need to be rich in order to own such trinkets; a man named Pinchbeck had perfected the art of making a metal which so closely resembled gold that the difference could only be detected by weight.

While the crinoline was in vogue it was worn by young and old; in

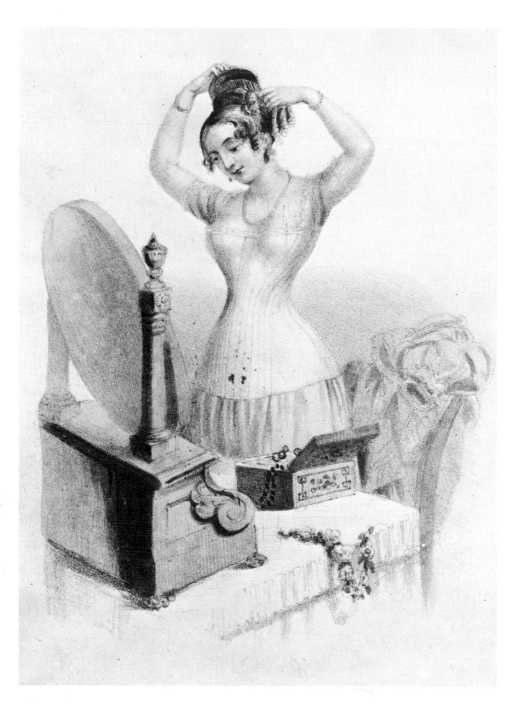

A Victorian beauty with a very small waist indeed. This print, delightfully entitled 'Mrs Nicholas Geary's Corsets', goes a long way towards explaining all those swoons and fainting fits.

the young it made the waist seem slender, while in married women it concealed pregnancy – for a time. It differed from the Tudor farthingale and from the Georgian panniers in that it was more flexible, being made of whalebone; it was in fact made like a birdcage, with hoops increasing in circumference as they went downward. Once again the well-dressed woman took up more room horizontally than she did vertically; new, armless chairs enabled her to accommodate her skirts. The crinoline needed careful management; one incautious move and the springy hoops could concertina, lifting both petticoats and skirts and revealing, most embarrassingly, that a lady had legs clad in 'unmentionables' (white linen drawers) with lace at the ankles.

Such dress, of course, was impractical wear for working women, but something approaching the fashionable outline could be attained by wearing two or three petticoats and having one's skirts cut full, and heavily pleated into the waist. And most women could afford a shawl. Shawls had originally come from Kashmir in India, but they were soon being made in Britain; a factory in Paisley turned out its own distinctive design. The best were woven of extremely fine wool and, though light, the square doubled into a triangle was very warm and, for wearing over full sleeves or lace berthes, more convenient than cloaks and coats.

There was a good deal of imitation – aping one's betters it was sometimes unkindly called in those class-ridden days – and this desire was encouraged by the invention of the sewing machine in mid-century, whereby ready-made clothes became cheaper and home dressmaking relatively quick and easy. The great name in the sewing machine business was, and for long remained, Singer. He took out his patent in 1851 and by the end of the century all but the very rich who preferred, or pretended to prefer, hand stitching, were wearing machine-made clothes. The first Singer sewing machine is in the Science Museum in London, and still in working order. An ancient Singer is often the only evidence of the machine-age encroachment in remote villages in India and Africa.

In England the invention both relieved and damaged those women who had stitched their lives away, either in dressmaking establishments or in their own homes, where, by taking in piecework, they could earn a little and at the same time look after their young children or their old relatives. They had always been cruelly exploited. Thomas Hood described their misery in his *Song of the Shirt*:

> With fingers weary and worn,
>     With eyelids heavy and red,
> A woman sat, in unwomanly rags,
>     Plying her needle and thread, –
>     Stitch! stitch! stitch!
> In poverty, hunger and dirt,
>     And still with a voice of dolorous pitch,
> She sang the 'Song of the Shirt'.

>     Work-work work,
>     My labour never flags;
> And what are its wages? A bed of straw,
>     A crust of bread, – and rags, –
> That shattered roof, – and this naked floor, –
>     A table, – a broken chair, –
> And a wall so blank, my shadow I thank
>     For sometimes falling there!

Now the machine could do the stitching, but it could not yet make buttonholes, or sew on buttons, so such finishing off jobs were still hired out at iniquitously low rates to the former seamstresses.

The contrast between the comfort of the middle and upper classes and the desperate poverty of masses of the working classes and unemployed horrified many foreign visitors to England in the nineteenth century. The comment of the American C. Edwards Lester in 1839 was typical: 'I have seen more magnificence than I ever wish to see in my own country, and more wretchedness than I ever supposed could exist.' Overcrowding was one of the chief horrors of the Victorian slum areas. Rows of houses, about eleven feet square, were built back to back with no garden or yard and only a narrow passage between one double row and the next. Inside large families would be crowded into each room 'with the walls unwhitewashed for years, black with the smoke of foul chimneys, without water, with corded bed-stocks for beds, and sacking for bed-clothing, with floors unwashed from year to year, without out-offices', as the reformer Edwin Chadwick

OVERLEAF These cottages, though probably damp and certainly over-crowded, would have been kept spotlessly clean.

graphically wrote in 1842. Another family would inhabit the dank cellar; in Liverpool in 1842 39,000 people lived in 7800 cellars.

The appalling sanitary conditions were the cause of much sickness among the poor. A typical street, Virginia Row in the East End of London, was visited by the Poor Law Commissioners in 1838:

> In the centre of this street there is a gutter, into which potato parings, the refuse of vegetable and animal matter of all kinds, the dirty water from the washing of clothes and of the houses are all poured, and there they stagnate and putrefy. . . . Families live in the cellars and kitchens of these undrained houses, dark and extremely damp. In some or other of these houses fever is always prevalent.

The filth was exacerbated by the scarcity of water. Some streets would have a single tap which was turned on for only a few minutes each day; others had no water at all and the inhabitants had to carry it back from afar or even pay for it by the bucketful. Edwin Chadwick realistically commented: 'The minor comforts of cleanliness are of course forgone, to avoid the immediate and greater discomforts of having to fetch the water.'

In the country conditions were less crowded, but the majority of farming cottages were 'deficient in almost every requisite that should constitute a home for a Christian family in a civilised community', according to the Rev. J. Fraser who inspected the eastern counties for a royal commission in 1867–70. 'They are deficient in drainage and sanitary arrangements', he continued, 'they are imperfectly supplied with water; such conveniences as they have are often so situated as to become nuisances; they are full enough of draughts to generate any amount of rheumatism; and in many instances are lamentably dilapidated and out of repair.'

For the labourers in both town and country wages were totally inadequate to feed and clothe a family and pay the rent. In rural areas poaching occasionally filled the bare larder but the laws against it were savage, and so were the man-traps which landowners installed on their property. Many cottages had no gardens or allotments, so the labourer's family were not even able to grow a few vegetables. Bread was still the staple diet of this class and gin still tempted the slum-

dwellers to pawn their sticks of furniture in order to win a night's forgetfulness of their misery. Men, women and children were forced to work such long hours to earn a meagre pittance that family life can have meant little more than the sharing of accommodation.

Not all the working class were in this desperate situation. The skilled artisans and mechanics could earn enough to rent a small terraced house, educate their children, dress respectably, eat oysters and take an occasional outing on the railway – but it was very difficult for the poorest classes to rise even this far from the depths of their poverty. One escape route could be domestic service. If a young girl was fortunate enough to get a post even as the lowest kitchenmaid, with a salary of less than ten pounds a year, she achieved an envied security. The work was hard but not nearly as hard as in the mines or factories,

A cottage interior. Next to the open fire, on which pots are cooking, is an oven of the 'beehive' type. Other features of interest are the baby-walker, and the bunk bed – perhaps for a farm labourer – reached only by a rope ladder.

and in the larger households she would probably be well-fed though the single maid-of-all-work in a small house was often meanly treated in this respect. And even a kitchenmaid had the hope of rising through years of honourable service to the heights of parlourmaid or cook, with twice the salary and immense prestige in her own small world.

English servants had a class structure all of their own and an American visitor, Elizabeth Bancroft, was amazed at its rigidity:

A lady's maid is a *very great* character *indeed*, and would be much more unwilling to take her tea with, or speak familiarly to, a footman or a housemaid than I should. My greatest mistakes in England have been committed towards those high dignitaries my own maid and the butler, whose

The servant problem. 'Followers' were not permitted by one's employer, and the cook has invented a sadly implausible excuse in an effort to explain away the presence of her young man.  .

DOMESTIC BLISS.

*Mistress.* "WELL, I'M SURE; AND PRAY WHO IS THAT?"
*Cook.* "OH, IF YOU PLEASE 'M, IT'S ONLY MY COUSIN WHO HAS CALLED JUST TO SHOW ME HOW TO BOIL A POTATO."

grandeur I entirely misappreciated and invaded, as in my ignorance I placed them, as we do, on the same level with other servants. She has her fire made for her, and *loaf* sugar in her tea, which she and Cates [the butler] sip in solitary majesty.

In her book on *Household Management*, published in 1861, Mrs Beeton estimated that a nobleman would employ twenty-five servants in a single establishment; a family with an income of £1000 a year would have a cook, upper housemaid, nursemaid, under housemaid, and a manservant; and even on £150 a year a family could afford a maid-of-all-work. It was in these small households that servants tended to be worst treated. There was no limit to the work that could be demanded, no hierarchy to appeal to, and often insufficient food, for a household which was struggling to keep a servant was not likely to be liberal in feeding her. Dickens gives a sad picture of the life of one of these skivvies in *The Old Curiosity Shop*:

One circumstance troubled Mr Swiveller's mind very much, and that was that the small servant always remained somewhere in the bowels of the earth under Bevis Marks, and never came to the surface unless the single gentleman rang his bell, when she would answer it and immediately disappear again. She never went out, or came into the office, or had a clean face, or took off the coarse apron, or looked out of any of the windows, or stood at the street-door for a breath of air, or had any rest or enjoyment whatever. Nobody ever came to see her, nobody spoke of her, nobody cared about her.

In the household hierarchy the nanny ranked high, even where there was a butler whom fellow servants must address as 'Mr'; he was replaceable, whereas a good nanny was not. Innumerable Victorian memoirs testify to the esteem in which the nanny was held, and to the lasting impression she left on the minds and characters of her charges. A very high-ranking naval officer was not ashamed to admit that, faced with an unexpected crisis, he always asked himself 'What would Nanny do?' Winston Churchill wrote of his nanny, 'Mrs Everest it was who looked after me and tended all my wants. It was to her I poured out my many troubles. . . .' Since Victorian families were large, and early marriage for girls still desirable, very often by the time the youngest member was ready for school or the schoolroom, the eldest

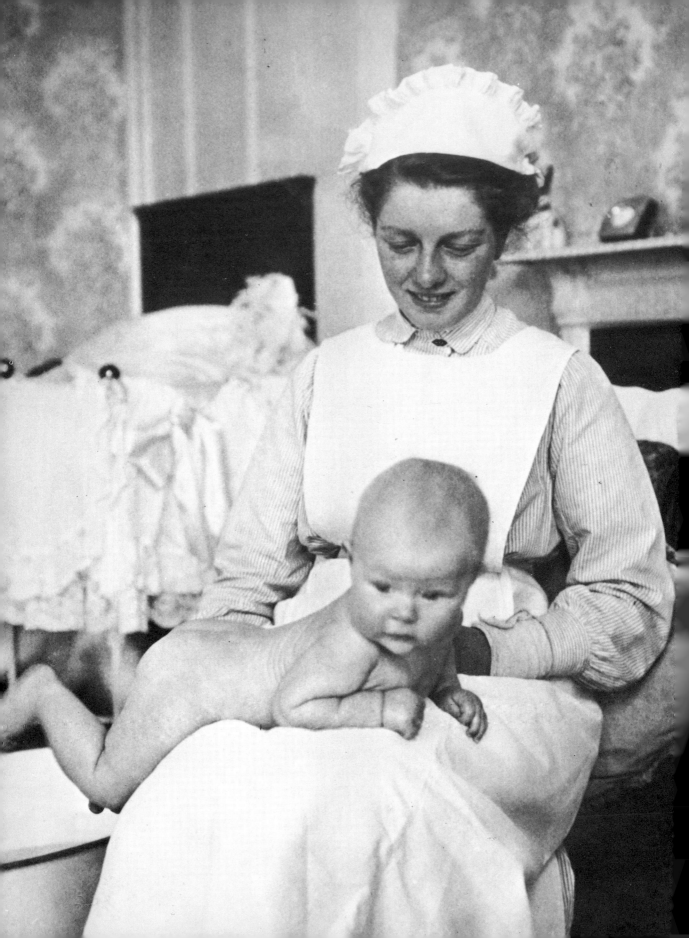

The nanny and the governess inhabited a strange kind of limbo that put them neither upstairs with the master and mistress, nor downstairs with the servants.

OPPOSITE A kindly-looking nanny with her young charge.

LEFT Richard Redgrave: *The Governess*, 1844. Pensive and sad, is she reading a letter from home?

had started a family elsewhere, and Nanny moved on. Often she was known by the name of the family she served; her name might be Emma Smith but within a given circle she would be known as Nanny Sutherland, or whatever. When she was past much active work – or the supply of young children had run out – she was seldom discarded; some little niche, some easy job could usually be found for her; and when she died she was often buried in the family plot.

Very different was the role and the fate of that other not-quite-servant of Victorian establishments – the governess. A few, but very few, memoirs mention her with affection, perhaps because few people even now hold teachers in high regard, and perhaps because her extremely anomalous position in the average household was not conducive either to sweet temper or sturdy self-confidence. The governess could be one of John Bull's daughters who had gained a modicum of education at the Female Academy and who could no longer be supported at home, waiting for marriage; more often she was the product of a poor parsonage. The Brontë sisters cannot be accepted as typical, since they were all possessed of genius, but at least they were articulate, and although Charlotte may have exaggerated slightly, her picture of the life of a governess shows it to be highly undesirable. Although Jane Eyre did eventually marry Mr Rochester, her employer, there are many pages concerning his patronizing, teasing and inconsiderate behaviour. Thackeray too paints a sad picture of the governess's life: 'She sits alone in the schoolroom, high, high up in that lone house, when the little ones are long since asleep, before her dismal little tea-tray, and her little desk, containing her mother's letters and her mementoes of home.' The governess was too high to take tea in the companionship of the servants' hall, but too low to be welcomed in the drawing-room.

By the end of the century maids in houses with bathrooms no longer had to run up and down with hip baths and footbaths because a large number of permanent baths had been installed. These were imposing structures, enclosed in the ubiquitous mahogany, standing high on clawed feet. However, it was usual to have a fire in the bathroom, so maids still had to carry fuel.

In the kitchen, however, labour was lightened by the advent of the gas cooker. A model was shown in the Great Exhibition of 1851, but gas was already in use for lighting streets in London and other progressive cities. The lamplighter – each lamp had to be kindled separately – became a familiar figure. Gas for lighting the interior of buildings was first tried out in factories and public buildings like the Houses of Parliament, where timid members thought it a dangerous innovation and expected the pipes to be hot. When it had proved itself to be harmless it was permitted to enter the ordinary household, displacing candles and oil lamps. In drawing-rooms and dining-rooms the gas fittings could be elegant brass pipes leading into glass globes, plain, frosted or engraved. In kitchens and passages and servants' bedrooms the pipe jutted straight out from the wall and the light was unshaded, bluish and bleak. Gas lighting never reached the country at all. Candles and oil lamps served there until the arrival of electricity.

OPPOSITE Running water made regular baths more of a pleasure for the bather and less of a physical effort for those who had previously had to convey the hot water. This print, dated 1896, is called 'The acme of solid enjoyment'.

The ultra-modesty of the crinoline which ignored the existence of anything below the waist, and of the poke bonnet which had become so large that the wearer's face seemed to be at the end of a tunnel, had changed in the late 1860s. Fashionable wear now was the bustle – a pad or a bunching up of material to emphasize the female posterior. Tight lacing remained, a small waist was still desirable, and the new fashion of dresses tightly stretched across the stomach made corsets a necessity. The bonnet had dwindled to a small, pancake-shaped hat which exposed the face. Hair was now dressed higher in front and at the side, though ringlets were still allowed to fall at the back. Since a fair complexion was still eminently desirable and freckles or sun-tan abhorred – and any obvious make-up a sure sign of loose morals – this was the age of the parasol. This pretty accessory had developed from the use, by Jonas Hanway in the previous century, of the umbrella, considered at the time to be highly eccentric. But the umbrella had caught on; specially wide and heavy ones were even manufactured for use in gigs. Further protection against wet weather became possible when Mackintosh discovered a way of using rubber for making cloth resistant to water, whereby, properly treated, the rubber would take on the shape of a mould; in America, one's waterproof footwear is still referred to as one's rubbers. As a substance it was rather fragile, until Charles Goodyear in America and Thomas Hancock in England discovered a method of making it harder and more resistant to wear and tear – the process known as vulcanization.

It had several results, one of the most valuable being the reduction of noise. People who now complain – with every justification – about the noise of traffic might cast a backward look to the time when all vehicles ran on iron-rimmed wheels and streets were so noisy that it was the custom to throw down straw in front of a house where someone was very ill.

One of the most eager consumer markets for the first rubber tyres was the bicycle business. The idea of a self-propelled, two-wheeled machine was not new, but the first ridable machine was actually made in Scotland in 1840. With unsprung seat and solid tyres it was rightly nicknamed a bone-shaker, and mounting and dismounting were not easy. The model produced in 1885 was called the Safety Model and soon women were riding it. Amelia Bloomer, a respectable married woman in New York, achieved notoriety by designing herself a garment eminently suited to the pastime – she rode her bicycle wearing trousers! Loose and full, gathered in at the ankle, her bloomers were the reverse of immodest, but even America, where women enjoyed much more freedom than in England, was mildly shocked. In Victorian England only the most courageous or outrageous women dared to wear them.

Towards the end of the century an attempt was made to free women of tight corsets and hampering skirts. A group of artists and writers, known as the pre-Raphaelites because they painted in the simpler style that prevailed before the High Renaissance and Raphael, advocated the natural waistline, a simple form of dress, uncluttered rooms, and a return to things made by hand. They were too late to avert the horrors of mass production but they did have a happy influence on design, and many a Victorian house was lightened by the delightful wallpapers produced by William Morris.

When Mrs Beeton's cookery book was published in 1861 the eating habits of ordinary households were approaching the style of the twentieth century. A recommended 'plain family dinner' was '1. Bubble-and-squeak, made with remains of cold beef. Roast shoulder of veal stuffed, spinach, potatoes. 2. Boiled batter pudding and sweet sauce.' Puddings were still much more popular than they are nowadays and there were endless varieties to choose from. In Eliza Acton's *Modern Cookery*, 1845, recipes ranged from 'The Poor Author's Pudding' made of bread, eggs, sugar and milk, to 'The Publisher's Pudding' which included macaroons, suet, almonds, cherries, raisins, candied peel, nutmeg, seven egg yolks, best cognac and over a pint of cream. 'This pudding can scarcely be made *too* rich' comments the poor author. It is interesting that in Eliza Acton's book lettuce and cucumber appear only as cooked vegetables. Sixteen years later Mrs Beeton still gives recipes for cooking cucumber but lettuce appears primarily as a salad vegetable: 'They are seldom served in any other way,' she writes, 'but may be stewed and sent to table in a good brown gravy flavoured with lemon juice.'

In spite of today's washing machines and refrigerators, many people would happily exchange a kitchen of this size for their modern matchboxes. Designed by Soyer, it is described as a 'miniature kitchen . . . suitable for middling-sized houses or cottages'!

Most housewives still made their own jams and custards, although Birds Eye custard powder appeared as early as 1840, and there were an increasing number of convenience foods in the shops, particularly when the canning process was perfected towards the end of the century. Margarine became popular as a substitute for butter and the use of refrigeration in steamships enabled vast quantities of meat to be imported from Australasia and America.

Men often ate at their clubs or a chop-house but respectable women did not dine out at restaurants, so the giving and receiving of dinner parties was an important social activity. 'Dinner, being the grand solid meal of the day is a matter of importance', wrote Mrs Beeton, 'and a well-served table is a striking index of human ingenuity and resource.' Indeed one can only admire the resource of a middle-class housewife who with the help of one or two servants was able to produce the following recommended dinner for eight people.

First Course
Mock Turtle Soup.
Fillets of Turbot à la Crême. Fried Fillet Soles and Anchovy Sauce.

Entrées
Larded Fillets of Rabbits. Tendrons de Veau with Puree of Tomatoes.

Second Course
Stewed Rump of Beef à la Jardinière. Roast Fowls. Boiled Ham.

Third Course
Roast Pigeons or Larks.

Rhubarb tartlets. Meringues. Clear Jelly. Cream. Ice Pudding. Soufflé.

It was still customary for ladies to retire after the meal, leaving the gentlemen to their port, but not as soon as in former times when, as Mrs Beeton said, 'the gentlemen of the company soon became unfit to conduct themselves with that decorum which is essential in the presence of ladies.' Nowadays things had improved so much that temperance was 'a striking feature in the character of a gentleman' and 'the very early withdrawing of the ladies from the dining-room is to be deprecated.' When the gentlemen rejoined the ladies in the drawing-room they might well amuse themselves by reading aloud favourite passages from a book or singing songs round the piano. The Victorians were less selfconscious than people today and thought nothing of crying in public over the death of Little Nell or declaiming stirring verses like 'The boy stood on the burning deck'. The tone deaf must have been at a sad social disadvantage for no respectable home lacked a piano and visitors brought along their party pieces to entertain the gathering. The taste for intimate music-making went right up the social scale. Tostig's *Goodbye* was a favourite with Queen Victoria and her daughters and the Prince of Wales declared he would 'travel the

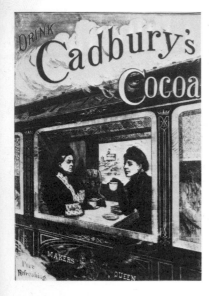

Advertising and public transport for all were two innovations which link the Victorian age with our own.

ABOVE The ultimate accolade was the royal approval.

RIGHT The new stations of the underground railway, which made journeys to and from the suburbs so much easier, were the ideal place to advertise one's products.

length of my kingdom' to hear *The Lost Chord* sung by a society lady, Mrs Ronalds.

Not all the Prince's amusements were so innocent and though he was, sometimes, a devoted family man, the tone he set for society at the opening of the twentieth century was very different from that of the home-loving Victoria. When the old Queen died in 1901 people felt, as they had on the death of the long-lived Elizabeth I, that they were witnessing the passing of a great era. But few can have imagined the extent of the changes which lay ahead.

OPPOSITE Victorian attitudes to morality were narrow-minded and, on the whole, unforgiving. F. R. Barwell's painting *Adopting a Child* reveals the plight of the unmarried mother in a society that lacked compassion.

# 7 The Equalizing Age

dward VII lived to enjoy only nine years of his long-awaited inheritance but his reign is looked back on as an era of its own, a decade of gaiety between the restraints of Victorian society and the cataclysm of the First World War. In fact, for the vast majority of people life continued along the Victorian pattern until the war. Poverty was still rampant in town and country, and living conditions were still appalling for millions of the population, although the construction of drains and sewers had improved health in the large cities. It was only the upper classes who could follow the extravagant, pleasure-loving pursuits of the new king, but this they did with such enthusiasm that the whole decade has shone with reflected brilliance.

Unlike his mother, Edward enjoyed pomp and ceremony and social life and under his influence London glittered with balls and parties and dinners. In the country it was a time of lavish weekend house parties when quantities of assorted guests drove down to the great houses to eat and shoot during the day, and eat and play cards in the evening. Edward encouraged extravagance in both food and clothes. He said openly that a meal of less than seven courses was not a dinner at all and reproved Lady Salisbury for appearing twice in the same dress. Consuelo Vanderbilt Balsan, who was Duchess of Marlborough in Edward's reign, wrote in her autobiography of the enormous demands made upon her wardrobe by a house party at Blenheim Palace:

To begin with, even breakfast, which was served at 9.30 in the dining-room, demanded an elegant costume of velvet or silk. . . . We next changed into tweeds to join the guns for luncheon, which was served in the High Lodge or in a tent. . . . An elaborate tea gown was donned for tea, after which we played cards or listened to a Viennese band or to the organ until time to dress for dinner, when again we adorned ourselves in satin, or brocade, with a great display of jewels. All these changes necessitated a tremendous outlay, since one was not supposed to wear the same gown twice. That meant sixteen dresses for four days.

As an example of the gargantuan meals that were served up, here is Sir Harold Nicolson's account of a mere breakfast:

Edwardian breakfasts were in no sense a hurried proceeding. The porridge was disposed of negligently, people walking about and watching the rain

OPPOSITE In the twentieth century the monarchy – aided by modern methods of communication such as radio and television – became more approachable, while the Welfare State assisted poorer people in obtaining a better standard of living. This painting by James Gunn, entitled *Conversation Piece at the Royal Lodge, Windsor* shows King George VI with Queen Elizabeth and their two daughters, Princess Elizabeth and Princess Margaret.

OVERLEAF The Edwardian age was truly the end of an era, and certainly after 1914 lazy summer afternoons like this were never quite the same again.

descend upon the Italian garden. Then would come whiting and omelette and devilled kidneys and little fishy messes in shells. And then tongue and ham and a slice of Ptarmigan. And then scones and honey and marmalade. And then a little melon and a nectarine or two, and just one or two of those delicious raspberries.

Edward VII died four years before the outbreak of the First World War and was succeeded by his son, George V. The new king had none of his father's flamboyance and love of luxury but his stalwart sense of duty and delight in domesticity made him much loved among the middle and working classes. Such sober qualities were suited to the grim years that lay ahead. When war broke out the house parties came to a sudden halt. Many of the great houses were turned into hospitals and all the young male guests departed to the trenches of Flanders. In the great houses as in the mean terraces, the greatest horror of this war was the appalling loss of life. In the first day of the Somme offensive 76,000 men died; 76,000 telegrams from the War Office devastated individual households after only one day's fighting. In many country churches memorial tablets record the end of a long family line when two or more sons were killed in the war.

The dearth of young men brought a degree of emancipation to many women when they were encouraged to step into the vacant jobs. Some became volunteer nurses, some donned breeches to work in the Land Army, many escaped from domestic service into shops, industry, and above all into the ever-hungry munition factories. Soon girls were earning more in a week than they had done in a quarter of a year, more than their fathers had done in a month. Some of them even bought fur coats – a subject for sour mockery.

The sensible precaution of rationing food was not taken soon enough. Nobody had visualized the submarine blockade which cut England off from her overseas larders. Rationing was by price, which was hard on the poor, and shopkeepers were supposed to distribute their scanty supplies equitably. Queues were the result, because cutting and packing small portions of such commodities as margarine took time, and because the sight of a few people waiting outside a shop attracted others. Many people joined queues without knowing exactly what they would be able to buy when they reached the counter. And

The First World War brought new status to women in that, for the first time, they were able to work in factories and earn decent wages.

rumour spread; there was butter, margarine, jam or tea, or a few potatoes at such and such a place. Families with many children benefitted from this hit-or-miss method, since the children could be distributed around a number of queues. In January 1918 *The Times* recorded a queue of 4000 people waiting to buy meat at Smithfield and a month later, at the London Central Market, 'queues began to turn up at 2 o'clock in the morning, and at 5.30, when the shops opened, no fewer than 2000 people were waiting.'

The people who ate best – even after rationing had been imposed, were those in the country. No amount of bureaucracy could account for every pig, every calf and every sheep in the country, and nobody but the most deliberately self-blinded idealist could expect that a man doing the work of three men – and a horse – was going to put everything he produced into the common kitty and draw no more than the townsman whose working hours and wages were fixed. In places, too, there was plenty of game; the men who had brought down grouse and partridges and pheasants before the war were now engaged with other targets.

Hunger and heartbreak were the main sufferings of civilians in the Great War. The Zeppelin raids brought a new terror to London and a few other cities but the damage and loss of life were tiny in comparison to the next war. And yet though the worst of the war was fought the other side of the Channel, the effect on the whole fabric of society was enormous. Class barriers were reduced, women proved their capacity in spheres outside the home and men who had suffered bitterly in the war expected their country to do something for them on their return. They were not prepared to sink back into the rut of poverty; they no longer 'knew their place'.

And yet despite ameliorative measures like the National Insurance which had been introduced in 1911, and despite the growing confidence of the trade union movement, poverty was to remain a feature of English domestic life throughout the inter-war years. The main cause was the Great Depression which kept unemployment between one and three million from 1920 to 1939. In some depressed areas a whole town or village would be living on unemployment benefit. The dole prevented the outright starvation of earlier ages, but it was quite inadequate to provide warmth and clothing as well as food.

Arthur Horner, first General Secretary of the National Union of Mineworkers, described in his autobiography his life as one of the unemployed in South Wales:

Most of the men had allotments and that would enable them to provide themselves with vegetables, but few had more than one – or at the most two – meals a day. We used to walk over the tips collecting lumps of coal. It was a point of honour never to buy anything if you could get it in other ways. We took wood from fences without any sense of shame. We would steal timber from the pitheads. And if a sheep could be enticed from the hillside, it would be killed and the meat divided among the people of the village. We shut the doors and windows while the mutton was cooking and we buried the fleece. We were not ashamed because we were being made outcasts by those who owned the means which could have given us a livelihood.

Housing was one area of deprivation in which the government did take action. Lloyd George had promised a land fit for heroes to live in and that hardly corresponded with the overcrowded and sub-standard houses which had caused concern even before the war. In some towns the average was two persons to a room. Subsidized housing was initiated in 1919 with the making of government grants to private builders, and in most cases this proved to be a very unsatisfactory system. So the local authorities took over and started to build council houses. At first they were reasonably cheap, and relatively spacious for land could still be bought at low prices. Most council houses were semi-detached, with a parlour, a living-room, a kitchen, three bedrooms, and an indoor lavatory. The bath was in the kitchen. There was a little garden at the front, and a larger one at the back. People who managed to obtain one of these houses were very fortunate and they knew it. Such houses usually went up in or on the fringes of towns; the rural areas were neglected since they were less overcrowded because at least 28 per cent of people who had left the land did not return to it. In the period between the wars only 2300 country families were rehoused.

In London and other large cities where less space was available flats were built in three- or four-storey blocks. Most were provided with a balcony on which young children could play, and where washing could be dried. On the whole the flat-dwellers were less happy and contented

ABOVE Early council houses, though small, were a great improvement on some of the slums which their tenants had just left.

OPPOSITE Interior of a house in a coal-mining village in the 1920s.

than those in council houses; they complained of the stairs, and of enforced proximity with neighbours who might, or might not, be compatible.

But the efforts of local councils only reached the tip of the iceberg in the housing problem. In 1936 Dudley Baker's report in the *Evening Standard* of 17 November on housing conditions in Merthyr, South Wales, reads depressingly like Victorian reports a century before: 'In two rooms in this tenement I found a family of eight – unemployed father, mother and six children. . . . The bedroom, dimly lit by a tiny window at one end, was completely filled by four beds in which the entire family slept. They pay 9s 6d a week rent for that.' And yet there are signs of hope in his article. Two of those six children attended secondary school; a hundred years before they would have been factory workers. And Baker noted that despite their poverty: 'Most of these people take a pathetic pride in their homes. Their furniture, old and shabby, is well-kept. Bedding, worn thin, cannot be replaced but it is clean. In tiny front patches grew chrysanthemums, and I saw a flower trained round a drainpipe which stank foully.'

The upper classes still took their pleasures seriously, in spite of the shortage of servants and other problems.

The beautiful town houses on several floors became less desirable after the war when high taxation made it less easy to afford servants, and when the supply of servants itself diminished due to the increase in other opportunities for female employment. Whole rows of select residential streets went on to the market and were converted into flats for single men and women who wanted to get away from home and for married couples who were saving for a house in the suburbs. Even the old basements were not despised; indeed they had the advantage of a separate entrance through what had once been the kitchen door. Many of these houses are still inhabited as flats today and it is clear how large rooms have been divided, for the cornices stop short at a wall and continue on the other side. Sanitary and cooking facilities have sometimes not improved since the 1920s; one lavatory and bathroom may serve several flats, and the kitchenette is often no more than a china sink and a gas ring behind a plywood partition or a curtain.

The great houses began to decline, domestically, with the First World War when they became impossible to staff adequately. Some owners were able to sell – though on an over-laden market – and stately homes became schools, nursing homes, hotels, or conference and training centres for large companies. Some private builders and rather fewer local councils would buy a big house and its grounds for development purposes, in which case the house itself was doomed, though its name might be remembered if the group of new homes was named after the old estate. Doomed to sink without trace were those – often splendid examples of the architecture and decor of their periods – which simply stood empty and rotted.

The National Trust, intent upon preservation, did what it could and saved a number, but its funds were limited and old houses, as the former owners knew, cost a great deal to keep in repair. The time came when the National Trust could not accept a house, however worthy, unless its owner could give it the equivalent of the old-fashioned dowry. Sometimes such arrangements included a provision for some part of the building to be reserved for the use of the original family, who often lived in greater comfort than any of their forebears had done, since the pylons now striding across the country enabled even the most remote place to enjoy the benefits of electricity. National Trust properties are open to the public and no deep psychological insight is needed to explain why places where some of the original family are still in residence attract more people than those which are merely show places. They have less of a museum atmosphere; they have doors marked 'Private' – and they exercise all the charm of Bluebeard's locked chamber; also, though the average visitor would go to the stake rather than admit it, snobbery is not dead. It is one thing to be told 'Queen Elizabeth slept here', but it is far more exciting to catch a glimpse of the descendant of Queen Elizabeth's host clipping a hedge.

The adaptation of households to life without plenty of servants was made easier by the increasing mechanization of cooking and house-work. Vacuum cleaners, electric irons, gas and electric cookers and refrigerators were all available in the 1920s, though they were only very gradually accepted as essential kitchen equipment, partly

A contrast in kitchens.

LEFT Cook is clearly mistress of her own private domain, and the silver-plated dish covers hang like trophies on the wall behind her.

ABOVE Not so many years later, it is the housewife who is filling the flan she has made herself with her own bottled fruit.

through expense and partly from tradition. By 1964 only 36 per cent of British homes had refrigerators.

Fashion in clothes had undergone many changes, but never one so revolutionary as that which the First World War brought about. In 1913 skirts were still so long that the middle-class woman, obliged to go out on her domestic or professional duty, edged her dresses with brush braid, a stiff and resilient substance which protected skirts from friction and dirt and was easily removed to be washed. She wore her hair dressed high, in Edwardian style, and the hat (without which no decent woman would appear out-of-doors) was pinned to the top of her head with formidable hatpins. She wore corsets and knee-length bloomers and also a garment known as a corset-cover or camisole, decorated with lace and ribbon. Her stockings would be in one of three colours, though they were seldom seen on: black for ordinary wear, brown for the country to match the heavy walking shoes and the tweeds; and white for tennis. Decent women wore no make-up; even the dabbing of a shining nose with a French device called *poudre-papier* was done surreptitiously.

Quite suddenly all was changed. Skirts crept up to knee level, and legs were emphasized by flesh-coloured stockings; corsets were discarded; women wore skimpy tubular dresses which either ignored the waist entirely or placed it at or below hip level, marked by a belt or a strip of braid or embroidery. Underclothes were reduced to a minimum with a mere suspender belt to hold up the stockings, and a flimsy combination of camisole and knickers known as camiknickers. Some young women wore a brassiere intended not to uplift and enhance the bust but to flatten and conceal it. For the first time in history busts were out. Hair became shingled or Eton-cropped and the tubular effect was emphasized by the cloche hat, a deep basin pulled so low that most of the hair and much of the face was hidden. 'By the late twenties', wrote Cecil Beaton, 'the accepted look had become as standardized as a prison uniform and there was scarcely any difference between styles for a child of eight, a flapper or a woman of eighteen, twenty or fifty-eight.' In fact it was a common complaint among young men that in a crowded place it was very difficult to pick out your own girl, since they all looked so much alike.

OPPOSITE Sanitation had grown by Edwardian times from non-existent through unpleasant to (almost) a thing of beauty.

# THE LAMBETH
## PATENT PEDESTAL
# "COMBINATION" CLOSET

## ADVANTAGES.

Front of Basin Lipped to form Urinal and Slop Sink when the seat is raised.

A water area equal to size of hole in seat, reducing the possibility of soiling basin.

Can be readily fixed, either square or across the corner of a room.

Self-contained, and all parts open to inspection.

Depth of water retained in basin, $1\frac{1}{2}$ ins.

It may be flushed by simple seat-action arrangement, or by a pull handle as shewn.

THE LAMBETH PATENT PEDESTAL "COMBINATION" CLOSETS are made both in STONEWARE, WHITE QUEENSWARE, and STRONG GLAZED WARE. The former being especially adapted for places where they are liable to rough usage, as, by reason of their great strength, they are not likely to be damaged.

THE WHITE QUEENSWARE, are specially well finished and suitable for higher-class work.

These Closets are strongly recommended for HOSPITALS, ASYLUMS, PUBLIC INSTITUTIONS, FACTORIES, TENEMENTS, MODEL DWELLINGS. Also MANSIONS and PRIVATE HOUSES, they are made both PLAIN & ORNAMENTAL, and can be supplied either with Turned-down (**S**) or Shoot-out (**P**) Traps.

## THE WATER CLOSET—SLOP SINK—AND URINAL COMBINED.
This Closet has been designed by DOULTON & CO., and was awarded

Every woman with any regard for fashion now used make-up, the powder rather pale, and the lipstick very red. Some girls were so lost to all traditional feelings of decency that they would re-powder their faces and re-redden their lips in full public gaze. The all-look-alike ambition was helped by a new process – permanent waving. The woman with naturally curly or wavy hair lost an advantage which had been hers through the centuries. At a price everybody who wished could attain a head of hair which resembled a ploughed field. The process was very expensive, so girls in offices and factories and even groups of housewives ran Permanent Wave Clubs, each contributing a small sum a week and taking turns to go to the hairdresser.

This was in line with the buy-by-instalment or hire-purchase fever which was sweeping the country. At first firms selling by hire purchase were quite unscrupulous in pressurizing housewives through door-to-door salesmen to take on commitments they could not afford, then reclaiming the goods the moment the payments faltered and selling them all over again. The customer did not even get back the instalments that had been paid. But gradually such firms were brought under stricter legal control and hire purchase became a respectable feature of domestic life. It was particularly useful for young couples who wanted to furnish their tiny homes with compact modern furniture and not the massive sideboards and dressers inherited from their grandparents. Hire purchase also became the accepted method of buying a house when building societies proliferated during the immediate post-war period and offered safe investment to depositors and mortages to borrowers.

Many of the new private houses were very badly built but in due course Housing Acts laid down minimum standards of space and comfort. The new houses sprawled in every direction around London and other major cities, introducing the suburban way of life where people worked some distance from their homes and spent many hours a week travelling. Often the new areas lacked any sense of identity and people looked back with nostalgia to the community life of the villages. It became increasingly difficult to earn a living in the country, and soon the country cottages were taken over and modernized by city people wanting to escape from it all at weekends.

OPPOSITE G. W. Joy: *The Bayswater Omnibus* (detail). On the buses there was not even the difference between first, second and third class to separate people.

Attitudes towards
children have
changed
tremendously in
the last half-
century.

RIGHT Over-dressed
Edwardian children
in a beautiful rocking
toy in their nursery.

BELOW Ramsgate
beach in the early
1900s.

LEFT The Second
World War disrupted
many families,
particularly London
ones whose children
were evacuated to the
country in the early
days of the war.

ABOVE The modern
baby in his eminently
practical stretch suit
– fifty years ago his
father would have
been horrified at the
thought of playing
with him!

The loss of a local identity was encouraged by the streets of suburban houses, pleasant enough but all alike, and the chain stores which sprang up in all major towns and displaced the little individual shops that had been a feature of town life since medieval times. The Co-operative Society, Boots and Woolworths were the first giants to appear. In the 1920s Woolworths sold nothing over sixpence, and though the store had a 'cheap and nasty' image it was a blessing to the poorer housewives who could buy mass-produced household goods at bargain prices.

Electricity was invading new or converted houses, first as a source of lighting, then of power and heating and gradually in the form of appliances. It also powered the new toy of fortunate households – the wireless. Its development had been encouraged by the war and afterwards sets were produced for public consumption. At first only one member of the family could hear through the headphones at a time, but as sets became more sophisticated the wireless became a much-loved feature of family life. News bulletins brought each household, however remote, into contact with national affairs, and entertainment and information were on tap for everyone. Both the rich and the poor laughed over Tommy Handley and listened affectionately to the Christmas broadcasts of George v.

In 1936 they heard the final bulletin of the old King's last illness: 'The King's life is drawing peacefully to its close.' George v had been a strictly constitutional monarch and his wife, Queen Mary, had been a model of all the proprieties and graces still valued by the older generation; but they had produced a son and heir, Edward, who was rather different, rather distrusted by the establishment. He was handsome and immensely popular, but not sufficiently conventional. Over his later life an enormous question mark hangs. Was his future decided on the day when, in dripping rain, he stood in a derelict mining village and said, 'Something must be done. Something shall be done', or was it when he made public his intention of marrying a woman who had already been through a divorce court and was prepared to do so again?

Perhaps we shall never know. And perhaps he will be remembered, apart from his all-for-love attitude which made him renounce the throne, for two very minor things. He made a soft shirt acceptable for evening wear, and he abandoned the formal presentation which had for so long made the entry of any girl into a certain social group something very special. Bedecked in traditional white satin and wearing the Prince of Wales' emblem – three white feathers – as a headdress, the debutantes moved in line, curtseyed, were given a word or a smile and then moved on to be photographed and thus established, socially, for as long as they lived.

Edward – for a brief time King of England, though he was never crowned – had no use for such pageantry; no official presentations, church attendance irregular, political feelings suspect. He could have fought the issue, but did not. The vast majority of ordinary people in England had chosen their mates and saw no real reason why a king should not enjoy a similar privilege. ('I fancied Joe the minute I saw him – lovely blue eyes he had.' 'Well, what's so bad about divorce – my Elsie had to get rid of her first, but we've been happy enough together.') A referendum taken in that gloomy autumn would have surprised the authorities very much.

It was quickly over; a king had abdicated: Long Live the King! And for the first time since Henry VIII had made, in rapid succession, four women of un-royal birth Queens of England, a woman of un-royal birth was crowned. Genealogists busied themselves trying to prove that the Duchess of York – now suddenly to be Queen – was descended from Robert Bruce who had briefly been King of Scotland. They wasted their time. Robert Bruce's claim to the throne of Scotland had been very shaky, and the woman who was now Queen of England needed no such propping up. She was enough in herself and continued to be so, years after ordinary women would have sunk back into dowagerdom. No Queen since the great Elizabeth, and no Queen Mother, ever enjoyed such universal popularity.

George VI and his Queen were soon plunged into the horror of a world war. From the very first it was realized that this was going to be total war, its nastiness penetrating every home in the country in the form of poison gas, or bombs, or even invasion. Food rationing was imposed from the first, and clothes rationing followed; anybody – great landowner or smallholder – who was not making the very best

ABOVE War-time in suburbia.

RIGHT Evacuation to the country did benefit town children in some ways.

OPPOSITE The exigencies of war-time food – no wonder the woman looks sceptical as the grocer does his best to recommend an unappetizing product.

"They call it Spring, Mummy, and they have one every year down here."

use of his acres faced a head-on confrontation with officials who were armed with extraordinary powers. There was conscription for all. In the Boer War and in the First World War women had served, but always as volunteers; now, everybody being equal, they could be conscripted too. Any woman not engaged in a job that kept the country and the war going or not engaged in the rearing of a child, could be called up and directed into either the armed forces or some useful civilian occupation. There were no fur coats in this war.

Food was more equitably distributed than it had been during the First World War, but there was less of it. In twenty years the population had increased and submarines were more efficient in stopping convoys. Millions of tons of food went to the bottom. A Ministry of Food was set up under Lord Woolton which exhorted people to 'Dig for Victory', but there was a limit to the amount of food which could be home-produced even when farmers were encouraged by subsidy to plough up some pasture land and when lawns and flowerbeds were turned into vegetable plots. Enormous care was taken to ensure that children, including the unborn, should suffer as little as possible. Pregnant women were allowed a little extra milk, as were young children. Local Food Offices issued supplies of a baby food formula as well-balanced as any specified brand; and orange juice and cod liver oil to ensure a supply of necessary vitamins. Restaurants were controlled to make sure that too much food was not deflected into the mouths of the rich. Main items were marked with a star and no customer could eat more than one starred item at a sitting. Later on no restaurant was allowed to charge more than five shillings for a meal; they made up their profits through the wine bill, but any person of limited means who was prepared to forgo the wine could enjoy the unaccustomed pleasure of eating at the most expensive restaurants in town! One austerity dish created by the chef of the Savoy Hotel was somewhat ambiguously christened 'Lord Woolton Pie'. *The Times* printed the recipe:

Take 1 lb. each of diced potatoes, cauliflower, swedes and carrots, three or four spring onions, if possible one teaspoonful of vegetable extract and one tablespoonful of oatmeal. Cook all together for 10 mins, with just enough water to cover. Stir occasionally to prevent the mixture from sticking. Allow to cool; put into a pie dish, sprinkle with chopped parsley, and cover with a crust of potatoes or wholemeal pastry. Bake in a moderate oven until the pastry is nicely brown and serve hot with a brown gravy.

The government, newspapers, magazines and radio plied housewives with good advice on how to make cakes without butter and sugar and pies without meat or fruit. People were encouraged to eat home-grown potatoes instead of bread (for which the grain was imported) and not to peel them:

> Those who have the will to win
> Cook potatoes in their skin,
> Knowing that the sight of peelings
> Deeply hurts Lord Woolton's feelings.

The traditional larged iced wedding cake was impossible with sugar rationed to 8 oz a week so it became acceptable to house the wedding cake in a cardboard superstructure covered in white satin. Eggs were so scarce that dried egg became a valuable substitute, though it is remembered with a shudder by those who suffered it. Very carefully prepared it was edible, though it bore little resemblance to any kind of egg. In places where food was produced in mass it was sorely ill-treated, emptied out on to a concrete floor, doused with pails of water and mixed by shovelling it about with a spade. The food authorities made valiant attempts to introduce another form of protein, whale meat – known as *snoek*. It was 'off ration' but its reception was mixed; some women were ready to swear that their husbands had eaten whale and said it was the best steak they had tasted in a long time; others repudiated it absolutely for when it was cooking it smelt of cod liver oil.

The remarkable thing was that organized austerity was, on the whole, beneficial to health; there was a marked drop in deaths from diseases caused by too much cholesterol – a product of fat – in the blood, and of ailments like diabetes which were associated with the consumption of too much sugar and starch. Fewer people suffered from obesity and its side-effects.

The dangers to civilians that this war would probably bring were fully appreciated by the government from the beginning. Everyone was issued with a gas mask, which they were instructed to carry with them all the time, and children and pregnant women were hurriedly evacuated to the country in expectation that the great cities would soon be devastated by bombs. Poison gas was fortunately one horror which never materialized. The bombs came, but not until several months of 'phoney war' had passed, by which time many evacuees, bored in the country or longing for their family, had returned home.

Nearly a third of London's families built an Anderson shelter in their gardens in which to take refuge during raids; it could be heated, according to government propaganda, by two large flower pots and a candle! 'Siren suits' were devised for shelter wear and special song books were sold for keeping up spirits during a raid. Flat dwellers could go to public shelters but there were not enough of these and many families slept regularly in the underground stations during the months of the Blitz. J. L. Hodson described the scene at Piccadilly station:

> If you can imagine a seaside resort on Bank Holiday, promenade and shops and sand littered with people sleeping out in grotesque attitudes, surrounded by suitcases and thermos flasks, with young children and babies worn out and sleeping, and transfer that picture to tube platforms, odd corners and staircases, you get a mild idea of what it is like.

When morning came the underground population stumbled sleepily homewards, wondering uneasily whether they still had a home or whether it had been reduced overnight to smoking rubble.

As the months passed some people became so accustomed to the nightly terror that they stayed at home. Colin Perry, an eighteen-year-old London boy in 1940, described in his diary one particularly bad raid:

> We crouched in the hall and screamer after screaming bomb pounded round us. Every moment we thought our last. The guns shook the ceilings and the earth spattered my window. Finally at 11 I turned in amongst that inferno. I was wakened throughout the night with crashing guns, zooming planes, bomb after bomb. Somehow we survived the night, and I was awakened again this morning at 8 by guns and the noise of Jerry, whose engines seem to throb in my brain.... The sirens kept people up for nearly ten hours last night, ten hours of hell.

During the war years nobody had wasted much attention on fashion. Clothes as well as food were rationed and all garments available to the general public were marked U for utility. They were adequate but not fanciful. Without filling in a form it was impossible to buy a blanket for the bed of a child who had outgrown its cot; how many people were there in the household, and how many blankets did they have already? What new clothes there were slightly reflected the neat, trim uniforms which so many young women were wearing. A pre-war garment could be given the square-shouldered look by a little judicious padding. There was talk of a wonderful new material, as fine as silk but far stronger; but every fibre of it was needed for making parachutes, and the possession of a pair of nylon stockings indicated some contact with America where such things were available. All but the few who had had well-stocked wardrobes before the war wore lisle stockings – or none at all – and as austerity increased women began to clump about in shoes with wooden soles. Evening Schools ran classes called 'Make Do and Mend', which encouraged ingenious conversions such as a pair of men's grey flannel trousers transformed into a boy's suit.

After the war there was the usual immediate rebound with the New Look in 1947 when the austere, rather military style gave way to softly rounded shoulders, nipped-in waists, and longer and fuller skirts. There was even an abortive attempt to reintroduce the crinoline, in a modified form, for evening wear – the skirt spread over a stiffened petticoat. The New Look had a short lifespan. Skirts became pencil-slim, and then shorter and shorter until in the 1960s came the mini which frequently ended only an inch or two below the buttocks. No fashion since Amelia Bloomer's cycling knickers had roused such an outcry. But when tights replaced the sordid sight of suspenders and white flesh, the mini became more acceptable and was donned by women of any shape and many ages.

Women clung to the mini long after fashion designers had decreed that skirts must be longer. The result was, in the seventies, a general decline in the force of fashion to tie women to a narrow style of dress. Clothes of any length and any fabric became worn at any time. Trousers became accepted wear for women of any age, and the tendency for girls to dress like boys led to 'unisex' fashion.

After the war the housing shortage was worse than ever. The government and local councils tried various solutions to the problem with pre-fabricated houses (built to last ten years but still going strong) and replacement of rows of Victorian terraces with high-rise council flats (bringing new problems of social deprivation). Successive rent acts have attempted to bring security to furnished and un-furnished tenants but the consequence has been a decline in the amount of accommodation available. Fifty per cent of British homes are privately owned but the cost of a mortgage in relation to income rose vastly in the early 1970s and made it very difficult for single or lower-paid people to buy their own houses.

The great achievement of the post-war years for domestic life was the setting up of the National Health Service in 1948. For the payment of an obligatory weekly contribution men and women earned the right to free medical and dental treatment for themselves and their depend-ents. Although the Health Service is under constant criticism it has succeeded in ensuring that a high standard of medical care is avail-able to everyone, whatever their financial position. The consequence has been, on paper, an increase in the recorded amount of ill-health for no-one now avoids consulting a doctor for fear of the expense.

Rationing continued for a few years after the war but by the 1950s the period of austerity was superseded by a rapid increase in the standard of living, particularly among the middle and working classes. Cars, televisions, record players, tape recorders, refrigerators and washing machines became increasingly commonplace; package hol-idays in exotic places came within the reach of the common man; children and teenagers were given or earned much more money and became a focus for advertisers. A popular song at the end of the 1950s expressed awareness of the great changes in living styles.

> It used to be fun, Dad and old Mum
> Paddling down Southend
> But now it ain't done, never mind chum,
> Paris is where we spend our outings.
> Grandma's trying to shock us all
> Doing knees-up rock an' roll
> Fings ain't what they used to be.

OPPOSITE In the present century women have made enormous strides forward. This photograph shows women coming jubilantly out of a polling booth during the first election at which women (but only those over thirty) were entitled to vote.

RIGHT The first television sets were regarded with great awe in the 1950s.

ABOVE and OPPOSITE New housing is not always a success. The motorway cutting through the suburbs splits communities and brings noise and dirt, while highrise flats, though cleaner and brighter than pre-fabs, are unsuitable for the very old and the very young.

The arrival of television proved to be a mixed blessing. For the sick or the lonely it was a geat comfort and solace but in too many households it discouraged any efforts by families to make their own amusements or even to make conversation. In the homes of addicts it governed family habits and mealtimes and even the arrangement of furniture in sitting-rooms, where the set became the focus which the hearth had formerly been. People with friendly and sociable natures were known to refuse invitations if the acceptance of them conflicted with some programme to which they had become attached, and all but the hardiest cinemas died after valiant struggles to keep going by cutting down staff and installing hot-dog counters. One could sit at home in comfort in one's slippers and be entertained with a choice of programmes.

Something new had come into family life – not merely entertainment – a personality from outside. The indefinable thing known as a TV personality commanded the respect and adulation which previous generations had bestowed upon royalty or people of genuine achievement. The owner of a TV personality need not be intelligent or even amiable, it was enough just to *be*. Its lucky possessor could swing elections, influence public opinion, start fashions, and of course, if he cared to hire himself out for the purpose, sell almost anything. Through the commercial television channel families were subjected to a ceaseless bombardment of advertisements, exhorting them to believe that using a particular brand of fish fingers would make them a perfect mother, that with a certain drink they would appear the best of hosts, that without a deodorant no-one would love them. No wonder materialism was said to be the religion of modern times.

One of the greatest changes in family life after the war was the continuing increase in the number of wives and mothers who went on working or returned to work. An outcry soon arose about the deprivation of latchkey children, but it was no new thing for children to come home to an empty house. The difference was that previously it had only been in those families where the wife needed to work. Now many middle-class women were enjoying responsible jobs which they did not wish to relinquish for the boredom of a mechanized kitchen, and the accepted pattern of domestic life was rudely shaken. In many

OPPOSITE Augustus John: *Washing Day,* 1912.

homes the wife took on a share of the financial responsibilities for the family without being released from any of the domestic burden, and even if a couple arrived home from work together the woman would go straight to the kitchen while the man put his feet up with a paper to await his supper. However, in recent years, this too has begun to change and some men exhibit a skill with brooms and babies which would have shocked their fathers.

Family life is thus adapting to the impact of the working mother. Another new development on the domestic scene – divorce – is a serious and increasing threat to family stability. There was a time when it took an Act of Parliament, a great deal of money and a great deal of scandal to achieve a divorce. And even when divorce became cheaper and easier there remained a social stigma, to avoid which many people lived miserable lives. Another potent factor was financial; a woman did not too hastily divorce the man who was her meal ticket. But as divorce has become still easier and more respectable, and as women have been given fairer financial settlements in divorce proceedings and are able to take up or resume careers, the rate of broken marriages has soared. The divorcees have the hope of a second marriage; the inevitable sufferers are the children.

And yet as we look back upon the passage of English domestic life we can only be grateful that we are privileged to live in the present, despite its materialism and its divorce rate. Who would exchange even a pre-fab for the cold wet cottage of a medieval peasant and how wonderful the range of frozen foods would seem to those who existed on bread and cheese. Even if we transport ourselves backwards into the upper classes we find plagues and pests, no sanitation, and the loss of many young children. Not only is domestic life so much more comfortable than it has ever been but it is so well organized that most domestic cares have left it. Cooking, washing and keeping warm are now made so easy that they absorb a tiny proportion of our lives in comparison with their demands upon our predecessors. We are left with the leisure to pursue amusement or learning, to explore the countryside our ancestors had no time to look at, to read the books they could not afford and to visit the great houses in which they worked as skivvies.

OPPOSITE David Hockney: *Mr and Mrs Clark and Percy*, 1970–71. Modern society is relatively classless, and people are judged by what they do rather than what they are. Ossie Clark is a well-known fashion designer; his wife wears the long skirt that is now acceptable at any time of day; and their home is typical of the uncluttered simplicity of modern interiors.

The kitchen is perhaps the heart of domestic life.

ABOVE The kitchen of tomorrow, as seen by a designer exhibiting in the 1949 Ideal Home Exhibition – a far cry from ration books and dried egg.

RIGHT Today's 'kitchen of tomorrow', as visualized by a Royal College of Art student. Considering that there are many people whose kitchens fall far short of the 1949 concept, we can only wonder what tomorrow's kitchen really will look like.

Nowadays there is no typical Mr Everyman and no typical Duke of
Plaza-Tora. Nobody is typical, or average, or ordinary or even
representative; but, since this book began with the great contrast
between the lifestyles of the Norman peasant and his overlord, the
Norman noble, let us end with the image of a modern family enjoying
the pleasures of a great country house open to the public, while the
owner of the place amiably and with undiminished dignity sells candy-
floss across the counter of the sweet stall.

# Further Reading

I read or consulted a large number of books while writing this one, and a selection of the most useful and interesting is given below.

Allen, Mea, *Plants That Changed Our Gardens,* David & Charles (1974)
Bagley, J. J., *Life in Medieval England*, Batsford (1960)
Barrow, W. S. *Feudal Britain*, Edward Arnold (1956)
Bentley, Nicholas, *The Victorian Scene*, Weidenfeld & Nicolson (1968)
Briggs, Susan, *Keep Smiling Through*, Weidenfeld & Nicolson (1975)
Brooke, Iris, *History of English Costume*, Eyre Methuen (1972)
*English Historical Documents*, vols. 5, 10, 11, 12, Eyre & Spottiswoode
Gregg, Pauline, *Economic and Social History of Britain 1760–1967*, Harrap (1972)
Hansen, H. H., *Costume Cavalcade*, Eyre Methuen (1972)
Hartley, Dorothy, *Food in England*, Macdonald (1955)
Hassall, W. O., *How They Lived* vol I, Basil Blackwell (1962)
Kerr, Jessica, *Shakespeare's Flowers*, Longman (1969)
Pearl, Cyril, *Victorian Patchwork*, Heinemann (1972)
Quennell, M. and C. H. B., *Everyday Life in England* vols 1–4, Batsford (1957–61)
Stenton, D. M., *The English Woman in History*, Allen & Unwin (1957)
Trevelyan, G. M., *English Social History*, Longman (1946)
Truman and Green, *Historic Costuming*, Pitman (1969)
Yarwood, Doreen, *English Houses*, Batsford (1966)
Ziegler, Philip, *The Black Death*, Collins, (1969)

Contemporary sources of particular interest (of which many editions exist) are Chaucer's *The Canterbury Tales, The Diary of Samuel Pepys, The Paston Letters* and *John Evelyn's Diary.*

# Acknowledgments

Title page. Illustration for 'Noon' from *Karl Fröhlich's frolicks with scissars and pen,* London, 1860. Victoria and Albert Museum.

4 The 'Metropole Kitchener'. Cambridge Folk Museum.

6 From *The Perfect Christmas* by Rose Henniker-Heaton. Weidenfeld and Nicolson Archives.

8 Department of the Environment, Crown Copyright Reserved.

11 National Monuments Record.

12, 14 Bodleian Library.

16 Kenneth Jagger.

18, 19, 20 British Museum.

23 Bodleian Library.

24, 25 Weidenfeld and Nicolson Archives.

29 Museum of London.

30–1 Roger Viollet.

33 British Museum.

36 Bodleian Library.

39, 40, 42, 46, 47 British Museum.

49 Mansell Collection.

50 Trinity College, Dublin.

53 Trinity College, Cambridge.

56–7, 58 British Library.

59 British Museum.

60 Trinity College, Cambridge.

62 Sussex Archaeological Trust.

65 Bodleian Library.

66 British Museum.

68 Bodleian Library.

69 British Museum.

70–1 (above and below), 71 (above) Bodleian Library.

71 (below) Sussex Archaeological Trust

73 Bodleian Library.

74 British Museum.

75, 76, 78 Bodleian Library.

80 British Museum.

83 (above and below), 84 (above) Cooper-Bridgeman Library.

84 (below) Weidenfeld and Nicolson Archives.

86 National Trust.

87 National Portrait Gallery.

88 Edwin Smith.

90 Weidenfeld and Nicolson Archives.

91 (above) National Monuments Record.

91 (below) Weidenfeld and Nicolson Archives.

94–5 Kupferstichkabinett der Oeffentlichen Kunstsammlung Basel.

97 Cooper-Bridgeman Library.

98 (above) Victoria and Albert Museum.

98 (below) British Museum.

101 National Portrait Gallery (Woburn Abbey Collection).

102, 103 Weidenfeld and Nicolson Archives.

104 Victoria and Albert Museum.

106–7 British Museum.

108, 109 Marquess of Bute.

112 By Gracious Permission of Her Majesty the Queen.

114 (left) Victoria and Albert Museum (Cooper-Bridgeman Library).

114 (right) Weidenfeld and Nicolson Archives.

115 Victoria and Albert Museum.

116 City Art Gallery, Manchester.

118 Mary Evans Picture Library.

119 Victoria and Albert Museum (Cooper-Bridgeman Library).

122 Mary Evans Picture Library.

124, 125 Weidenfeld and Nicolson Archives.

127 (above and below) Mary Evans Picture Library.

128 Weidenfeld and Nicolson Archives.

130  Society of Antiquaries.
132, 134  Cooper-Bridgeman Library.
136  Weidenfeld and Nicolson Archives.
137  Kenneth Jagger.
138  Josiah Wedgwood & Sons Ltd.
139  Weidenfeld and Nicolson Archives.
141  Cooper-Bridgeman Library.
142–3  National Gallery of Ireland
   (Cooper-Bridgeman Library).
144  Cooper-Bridgeman Library.
146  British Museum (Cooper-
   Bridgeman Library).
147, 149  Weidenfeld and Nicolson
   Archives.
150  Tate Gallery.
153  Weidenfeld and Nicolson Archives.
154–5  National Gallery.
156  Victoria and Albert Museum
   (Cooper-Bridgeman Library).
157  Cooper-Bridgeman Library.
160  (above) Weidenfeld and Nicolson
   Archives.
160  (below) Tate Gallery.
161  Weidenfeld andNicolson Archives.
164  and endpapers British Museum
   (Cooper-Bridgeman Library).
166  Victoria and Albert Museum
   (Cooper-Bridgeman Library).
168  (above) British Museum.
168  (below) Weidenfeld and Nicolson
   Archives.
170  Guildhall Library.
172  British Museum.
175  Mansell Collection.
177  (above) C. B. Radcliffe Collection.
177  (below), 178–9 Cooper-
   Bridgeman Library.

181  (above) Richard Green (Fine
   Paintings).
181  (below) Tate Gallery.
182–3  American Stock Photos.
185  Weidenfeld and Nicolson Archives.
188–9  Greater London Council.
191, 192  Mansell Collection.
194  Richard Dennis Collection.
195  Victoria and Albert Museum
   (Cooper-Bridgeman Library).
197, 200  Mansell Collection.
202  Cadbury Bros., Bournville.
203  London Transport Executive.
204  M. Newman Ltd.
206  National Portrait Gallery.
209–10  Mrs. J. R. Ede.
211  Imperial War Museum.
214  Greater London Council.
215  National Coal Board.
216  Weidenfeld and Nicolson Archives.
218  Greater London Council.
219  Mansell Collection.
221  Weidenfeld and Nicolson Archives.
222  Museum of London (Cooper-
   Bridgeman Library).
224  (above) Mrs O. N. Jeffcock.
224  (below) Aerofilms.
225  (left and right), 228 (above and
   below) Weidenfeld and Nicolson
   Archives.
229  Imperial War Museum.
234  Radio Times Hulton Picture
   Library.
236  (above and below) Keystone.
239, 240  Tate Gallery.
242  (above) Mansell Collection.
242  (below) Keystone Press Agency.

Picture editor Julia Brown.

The publishers have taken all possible care to trace and acknowledge the sources of illustrations. If any errors have accidentally occurred, we shall be happy to correct them in future editions, provided that we receive notification.

Acton, Eliza, 199
advertising, 235, 238
Aesop's *Fables*, 96
air raid shelters, 232
Albert, Prince, 171, 175
ale, 28, 32, 99, 156
Alfred, King, 13, 21
allotments, 213
Andreas Franciscus, 99
Anne, Queen, 117, 129, 133
architecture
    Georgian, 135–6
    Jacobean, 82, 113
    medieval, 11–13, 48
    Norman, 10–11
    Queen Anne, 133
    Tudor, 67, 82–8
    twentieth century, 223–6, 235
    Victorian, 174
Austen, Jane, 169

*Babees' Book, The*, 72 3
bacon, 15, 99
Bacon family, 81
bakehouse, 10
Baker, Dudley, 115
Baker, Mrs Samuel, 181
Bancroft, Elizabeth, 192
Bath, 162, 164
bathing, 59–60, 162, 196, 213
Baxter, Richard, 117
Bayeux Tapestry, 37
Beale, Dorothea, 181
bear baiting, 77
Beau Brummell, 159–62
bed, 11, 107, 110
Bedlam, 151
Beaton, Cecil, 220
Beeton, Mrs, 193, 199, 201
bench, 32, 82
bicycle, 198–9
Black Death, the, 60, 79

bleaching, 36–7, 105
Blenheim Palace, 133
Bloomer, Amelia, 199
bodice, 100
*Boke of Husbandry*, 110
Boorde, Andrew, 89
Boswell, James, 158
Brahmah, Joseph, 162, 163
brasses, 58
bread, 19–22, 99, 190
breakfast, 32, 110, 207–10
brick buildings, 48, 88
Brighton, 164
Browning, Elizabeth Barrett, 181
Browning, Robert, 181
Buckingham Palace, 162
building societies, 223
bull baiting, 77
Bull, John, 165–7
Burney, Fanny, 162
Buss, Frances, 181
butter making, 63–4, 110

Campbell, Colen, 136
Campion, Thomas, 96
candle, 15, 26, 82
candle making, 26
*Canterbury Tales, The*, 47, 68
carding, 34
cards, 207
castle, 10–11
Caxton, William, 75, 96
Cecil, Robert, 82
Cecil, William, 96
Chadwick, Edwin, 187, 190
chain stores, 226
chair, 32
Chambers, Sir William, 137
Charles I, King, 115, 117
Charles II, King, 118, 130
Chaucer, Geoffrey, 47, 68, 75
cheese, 64, 99

cheese making, 64–7, 110
Chepstow Castle, 10
chess, 41
chest of drawers, 88–9
child labour, 38–9, 68, 72, 145–6, 164–5, 191–2
Chippendale, Thomas, 137
chocolate, 120, 122
Churchill, Sir Winston, 193
cider, 28, 99
cinema, 238
*City Letter Book Regulations*, 47
Civil War, the, 113, 115
club, 200
cock fighting, 77
coffee, 120, 122
coffee house, 120, 126
Colchester Castle, 10
commuting, 223
*Compleat City and Country Cook*, 151
*Complete Body of Architecture*, 135
conscription, 230
cooker, gas, 196
corset, 115, 198, 199, 220
costume
    Edwardian, 207
    eighteenth century, 159, 167
    Jacobean, 113–14
    medieval, 46, 55–8
    Norman, 35, 37–8
    Puritan, 117
    Restoration, 118–19
    Tudor, 100–5
    twentieth century, 220, 233
    Victorian, 184–6, 199
cottage, 9, 12–13, 38, 39, 138–40, 190, 223
cottage industry, 145
council houses, 213, 214
crinoline, 184–5, 198
Cromwell, Oliver, 115, 117
Cromwell, Thomas, 81

crusades, 44, 46–7
Cummings, Alexander, 162
cup, 27–8
cupboard, 27, 82
curfew, 13
curtains, 11
cutlery, 28

damper, 13
Defoe, Daniel, 145
Dickens, Charles, 193
Dickson, R. W., 139
dinner
    evening, 200–1, 207
    midday, 32, 110, 199
dinner party, 200–1, 207
dining-room, 85
disease, 34, 52–5, 152, 190, 231
divorce, 241
*Domesday Book*, 10, 16, 28
Dowland, John, 96
draughts, 41
dripping, 25
drunkenness, 152, 156–8
Dutch influence, 132–3
dyeing, 35–7
*Dyetary*, 89

*Earnest Appeal for Mercy to the Children of the Poor, An*, 140
Edward the Confessor, King, 13
Edward I, King, 60
Edward II, King, 60
Edward VI, King, 81
Edward VII, King, 201, 205, 207, 210
Edward VIII, King, 226
egg, dried, 231
Eleanor, Queen, 29, 45
electricity, 226
Eliot, George, 165
Elizabeth I, Queen, 89, 100, 106, 111, 113, 120, 205, 217

embroidery, 37, 100
employment, 78–9, 106, 145–6, 186–7, 190–1, 210, 213, 216, 238–41
enclosures, 67, 105, 140
Erasmus, 85
Evelyn, John, 128–9, 130

factories, 145
fair, 75, 77–8
farthingale, 100, 113
feasting, 75, 99, 123–5
feudal system, 13, 61–3
fire
    destruction by, 9, 13, 48, 113
    domestic, 10
Fire of London, the, 130
fireplace, 10, 16
fish, 32–4
flats, 213–14, 216, 235
food
    adulteration of, 148
    fresh, 17–18
fruit, preserving, 122
Fry, Elizabeth, 181
furniture, 13

gambling, 158
garde-robe, 51–2
gardens, 92–3, 132–3, 137–8
    pleasure, 120
gas, 196
George IV, King (Prince Regent), 159
George V, King, 210, 226
George VI, King, 227
gin, 152–7, 191–2
Goodyear, Charles, 198
goose, 67–8
governess, 195–6
Great Exhibition, the, 196
guilds, 68, 81

hair, 40–1, 55, 115, 120, 158–9, 185, 198, 220, 223

hall, 11, 82
Hampton Court, 82, 93
Hancock, Thomas, 198
Hanway, Jonas, 140, 198
Hardwick Hall, 85
Harington, Sir John, 89
Harrison, William, 107
Harvey, William, 129
Hatfield House, 82
hawking, 75
head-dress, 35, 46, 55, 58
Henry II, King, 29, 43–4, 45
Henry IV, King, 60
Henry V, King, 60
Henry VII, King, 81, 82
Henry VIII, King, 58, 93, 103, 106, 227
Hepplewhite, George, 137
hire purchase, 223
Hodson, J. L., 232
Holkham House, 135
*Home Book*, 176
homespun, 34, 37
honey, 22
Hood, Sir Thomas, 187
Horner, Arthur, 213
hostel, 38
Houghton Hall, 136
*Household Management*, 193
hunting, 17, 75

insurance, fire, 130

James I, King, 82, 99, 111, 113, 130
James II, King, 130
Jesty, Benjamin, 152
jewellery, 100–3, 117, 120, 184, 207
jug, 29

Kalm, Peter, 167
Kent, William, 135, 137
kitchen range, 13, 163–4

labour saving devices, 217–20, 235
Land Army, the, 210
lantern, 26
Latimer, Bishop, 81
leisure, 40–1, 75, 85, 93, 96–7, 117, 126,
    238, 241
linen
    household, 37, 88
    personal, 37
Lloyd George, David, 213
London, Tower of, 10
long gallery, 85
luxuries, 235

Mackintosh, Charles, 198
mahogany furniture, 137
Malory, Sir Thomas, 96
manor house, 11
manor, lord of the, 13, 17, 18–19, 39, 45,
    61–3
margarine, 200, 212
market, 47, 77
Marlborough, Duchess of, 207
Mary I, Queen, 99
Mary Queen of Scots, 120
Matilda, Queen, 43
May Day, 77
maypole, 77
mead, 28–9
meat, 14–15, 17, 24–6, 99, 167, 200
    preserving, 15, 17, 34
medicine, 52–5, 129, 151–2, 171, 235
Mereworth, 135
Michaelmas, 68, 78
milk, 17, 148
minstrels' gallery, 82
Mirfield, Johannes de, 53
Modern Cookery, 199
Mompesson House, 133
monasteries, dissolution of the, 106
More, Sir Thomas, 93
Morley, Thomas, 96, 97

Morris, William, 199
Morte d'Arthur, 96
mourning, Victorian, 175–6
music, 41, 96–7, 126, 201–5

nanny, 193–5
National Health Service, 235
National Insurance, 212, 235
National Trust, the, 217
needlework, 37
Nicolson, Sir Harold, 207
Nightingale, Florence, 181
Norman Conquest, the, 9

oak furniture, 88
Ordericus Vitalis, 10
oven, 10, 21–2, 67, 164

Palladio, 135
panelling, 88
parasol, 198
Pasqualigo, 103
Paston Letters, The, 74–5
pastry, 22
Pavilion, Brighton, 162
Pepys, Samuel, 120, 122–8, 129
perry, 28
Perry, Colin, 232
petticoat, 100, 113–15, 159, 186
Pevensey Castle, 10
pewter, 107
Philip, King of Spain, 99
photography, 175
Piccadilly, 105
Piers Plowman, The Vision of, 79
pig, 13, 14–15, 166
plague, 60, 129
Plague, the Great, 129
Plaine and Easie Introduction to
    Practicale Musicke, 97–8
plaster, 88, 113
plays, 75

poaching, 190
Poor Law, the, 106
potato, 99, 212
poverty, 106, 140, 187–90, 207, 212–13, 214
prefabricated houses, 235
preserves, 122, 200, 212
printing, 75, 96
privacy, 11, 85
Puritanism, 117–18, 129

Quarter Day, 78
Quenell, Thomas, 107

Radcliffe, Dr, 129
radio, 226
railway, 191
Raleigh, Sir Walter, 99
rationing, 210–12, 227, 230, 235
religion, 172–3
Renaissance, the, 81
Restoration, the, 118, 122, 129
Richard I, King, 44
Richard II, King, 59, 60
Richard III, King, 60, 81
Robinson, Sir Thomas, 136
Robinson, Thomas, 163
ruff, 105, 113
rush dip, 15, 26
rushes, 26, 82–5

St Bartholomew's Fair, 77
salt, 15–17, 27, 32, 64
Samson, Abbot, 34
sanitation, 48–52, 89–92, 162–3, 190, 207, 216
scent, 58–9, 82
schools, 81–2, 94, 161, 172
scribe, 75
scurvy, 17–18
servants, 32, 68, 85, 125, 169, 191–3, 216
sewing machine, 186–7

sheep, 63, 105
Sheraton, Thomas, 137
Sheridan, R. B., 158
shoes, pointed, 55
shooting, 207
skirt, 55, 58, 100, 113–15, 159, 184–6, 198, 199, 220, 233
smallpox, 54, 152
Smiles, Samuel, 172
soap, 37
solar, 11
spices, 23–5
spinning, 34–5, 110
spit roasting, 25–6
spring cleaning, 92
stately homes, 217
Stephen, King, 43, 48
stone buildings, 9–10, 48
storage
    food, 15
    garments, 51–2, 88–9
sugar, 22, 122, 148
supper, 32, 110

table, 27, 82
tablecloth, 27
tax, 43, 132, 166, 216
tea, 120, 122
teeth, 148–51
television, 238
tennis, 93
Thackeray, W. M., 196
theatre, 126
Theobalds, 82
time of day, 32
Tintinhull, 133
tithe, 20
toast, buttered, 167
tobacco, 99–100
topiary, 92
tournaments, 75
towns, 47, 52, 81, 145–8, 187–90

Townshend, Lord, 140
Tradescant, John, 133
travel, 38, 223
trousers, women's, 210, 233
Tull, Jethro, 140

umbrella, 198
*Utopia*, 105–6

Victoria, Queen, 171, 175, 201, 205
vitamins, 17–18

walnut furniture, 137
Walpole, Horace, 137
Walpole, Sir Robert, 136
wardrobe, 51–2, *see also* garde-robe
Wars of the Roses, the, 81
water, 28, 52, 187, 190
water closet, 87, 162–3
wattle and daub, 16
weaving, 34, 110
well, 28, 52
Wellington, Duke of, 162

whale meat, 231
*White Book of the City of London, The*, 48
wig, 120, 158, 159
William I, King, 13, 24
William II, King, 55
William of Dene, 61, 63
William of Malmesbury, 55
William and Mary, King and Queen,
    130
window, 85
window tax, 132
Windsor Castle, 89
wine, 28, 29
Winter Parlour, 85
wireless, 226
Wolsey, Thomas, 81
wood inlay, 137
wooden buildings, 9–10, 11–13, 48, 113
wool, 34, 76, 117
Woolton, Lord, 230
workhouse, 140, 165
World War I, 210–12
World War II, 227–32
Wren, Sir Christopher, 130